LIFE IN ANCIENT ROME

LIFE
IN
ANCIENT
ROME

Reader's
Digest

Published by
THE READER'S DIGEST ASSOCIATION LIMITED
London   New York   Sydney   Montreal

IMPERIAL CURRENCY   A gold coin shows
the head of the emperor, Diocletian.

DAILY BREAD   In a wall-painting from Pompeii,
a baker serves loaves of bread to his customers.

LIFE IN ANCIENT ROME
Edited and designed by Toucan Books Limited
Sole author: Robert Sackville West
Consultant: Tony Cubberley

First edition copyright © 1996
The Reader's Digest Association Limited
11 Westferry Circus, Canary Wharf,
London E14 4HE

www.readersdigest.co.uk

Copyright © 1996
Reader's Digest Association Far East Limited
Philippines copyright © 1996
Reader's Digest Association Far East Limited
All rights reserved

Reprinted 2000

Printing and binding: Printer Industria Gráfica S.A.,
Barcelona
Separations: Rodney Howe Limited, London
Paper: Perigord-Condat, France

ISBN 0 276 42128 0

Front cover (clockwise from top left): Food being
served at a banquet; portrait of a couple, Pompeii;
fruit-gathering; charioteer; wood and ivory toiletry
set; lady with her servants; bust of Pompey.

Back cover (clockwise from top left): Cameo
portraits of emperors and their wives; tombs outside
the wall of Pompeii; woman gymnast; butcher's
shop; milling flour.

Page 1:   In this wall-painting from the 2nd century
AD, the Romans relax with a ball game – an activity
that was particularly popular at the public baths.

Pages 2-3:   The imperial family process around
the walls of the Altar of Augustan Peace,
a monument built to celebrate the greatness of
Rome's first emperor.

CONTENTS

LIFE OF LEISURE In this relief,
a servant attends her mistress.

TABLE SCRAPS A mouse nibbles at a
nut among the leftovers from a
Roman meal, in this floor mosaic.

GREEK STYLE
This bronze statue of a
boy removing a thorn
from his foot was
influenced by ancient
Greek art.

HARD MAN A marble
bust of Julius Caesar,
a brilliant military
commander and a
political genius.

WHO WERE THE ROMANS?

Over the course of a thousand years, the people of Rome evolved from simple farmers

into the most cosmopolitan city-dwellers of the ancient world.

Their legacy is still alive in the languages, literatures, laws and architectural landmarks of today.

FOR A TOURIST TODAY, wandering around the Roman Forum, few experiences are more immediate than the sight of some green streaks in the street beside a building called the Basilica Amelia. These are the remains of copper coins that melted in the fires which devastated Rome, when the city was sacked by the Goths in AD 410, and were seared into the marble pavement. The fires have long since subsided, but the embers of the Roman Empire continue to glow around the world.

The civilisation of ancient Rome, which lasted from around the 6th century BC to the 5th century AD, has marked the Western world more deeply than almost any other past civilisation. From roads that still march arrow-straight across the European landscape to the towering arches of Roman aqueducts in places such as Segovia in Spain, the numerous visible traces the Romans left behind survive to this day as impressive memorials to their one-time might and engineering prowess.

Spreading its influence even wider, their language Latin, until relatively recent times a near-universal language of scholarship, gave birth to the modern world's Romance family of tongues, from Romansch spoken by some 50 000 people in Switzerland and northern Italy, to Spanish spoken by more than 150 million people worldwide; even English owes much of its vocabulary and syntax to Latin via French. Roman law, meanwhile, was a basis for the legal systems of nations and

territories as different as Scotland, Quebec, Argentina, and even Japan; while senates in countries from Italy to Ireland, and from the United States to Chile testify to the lasting influence of Roman political structures.

In their own time, the Romans' achievements were no less remarkable. They were the only people who have ever succeeded in uniting the whole of the Mediterranean coastline under a single ruler. When the emperor Trajan died in AD 117, the Roman Empire had reached its greatest extent. It stretched from Britain to North Africa and from Spain to the Caspian Sea, covering some 2 million sq miles (5 million km²) and counting around 100 million people as its subjects. Yet it had been built by just one Italian city, whose population even at its peak barely exceeded a million.

At the same time, the Romans left a more intimate, personal legacy. They were the first letter-writers of the ancient world, and the

ROMULUS AND REMUS A bronze statue, dating from the 5th century BC, shows the legendary twins Romulus and Remus being suckled by a she-wolf.

A TALE OF THREE CITIES

NEITHER Pompeii nor Herculaneum was a particularly important city. But the fact that they were destroyed suddenly rather than after long years of neglect, decay and abandonment has given us our most vivid record of what everyday life was like in a Roman town. The discovery of medical kits, coins, toys, tools, pottery, pavement graffiti, mosaics and wall-paintings have all contributed to an uncannily clear snapshot of life on the morning of August 24, AD 79.

This was when Mount Vesuvius erupted with ten times the intensity of the Mount St Helens eruption in 1980. A column of gas and volcanic debris was blown several thousand yards into the air, darkening the sky and precipitating a deluge of ash and cinders some 20 ft (6 m) deep over Pompeii. Most of the inhabitants of Pompeii died that day, crushed under collapsing roofs or asphyxiated by poison gas. Their bodies were trapped inside the layer of ash which solidified as it cooled. The bodies eventually decomposed, leaving a hole where

FORCE OF NATURE A photograph of the eruption of Vesuvius in 1879 gives some idea of the force which destroyed the city of Pompeii in AD 79.

the flesh had once been. Archaeologists have injected liquid plaster or, more recently, resins into these cavities to produce the terrible casts of people transfixed at the moment of death almost 2000 years ago.

When the build-up of pressure in Vesuvius had subsided, the cone of the volcano collapsed onto itself, and molten lava poured through the openings and down the slopes, burying nearby Herculaneum beneath rivers of volcanic mud some 33 ft (10 m) deep. Ostia, the ancient port of Rome, is also remarkably well preserved. Here, the decline of the city in the 4th century AD was followed by the gradual silting up of the harbour and the burial of the buildings beneath the sand.

MOMENT OF DEATH A plaster cast captures a man in his death throes. Huddled against a wall, he presses his cloak against his mouth in an attempt to prevent suffocation.

RUINS RESTORED French architect François Mazois began to restore Pompeii in 1809; his 454 drawings of the lost city were published some 20 years later.

survival of much of their correspondence has enabled later generations to get to know some of them as individuals: from the great orator and statesman Cicero, living during the last years of the Roman Republic in the 1st century BC, to the administrator Pliny the Younger whose letters give a clear idea of the attitudes of the wealthy during the heyday of the Empire in the 1st century AD. Pliny's correspondence gives a balanced account of the day-to-day activities of the aristocratic senatorial class, their public-spiritedness, their faith in the law, their tolerance, and above all their great sense of what was right and wrong. It paints a picture of a very proper world, rather than the crumbling and corrupt civilisation portrayed both by contemporaries and by later historians, who read the seeds of Rome's eventual downfall in the annals of the 1st century AD.

A BRIEF HISTORY OF ROME

According to legend, Rome was founded in 753 BC by Romulus, the city's first king, who had been nursed from birth by a she-wolf. It is archaeological fact, however, that tribes of shepherds had been living in the hills around Rome for centuries before 753, converging in the marshy valley where the Forum now stands for meetings and markets. In the 7th and 6th centuries BC, the Etruscan kings of Rome – including Tarquinius Priscus, Servius Tullius and Tarquinius Superbus – drained the marshes and built the first public buildings, temples, shops and a market square. In 509 BC the Romans rebelled, expelled their Etruscan rulers and established a republic which was to last almost another 500 years. Two consuls of equal status were elected by the citizens

TWO CULTURES Celsus presented the Greek city of Ephesus, in Asia Minor, with a library. This statue, symbolising his virtue, acknowledges the symbiosis of Greece and Rome.

to serve for one year only. One consul would go to war with Rome's citizen-army when danger threatened, while the other stayed to run the city. The consuls exercised power on behalf of the Senate, drawn from the city's aristocracy, and were supported in their tasks by several other magistrates elected by the people.

The other Latin tribes in central Italy gradually came to acknowledge Rome's leadership, and by 264 BC Rome was in command of the whole of the Italian peninsula south of the Po river. One of the ways in which it maintained its control over conquered territories was by establishing new communities, or colonies, with constitutions modelled on that of Rome. A consequence of this was that as Italy became more Roman, Rome itself became more Italian – with the citizens of the colonies exercising influence in the capital itself. It was a policy that the Romans were to adopt as they expanded overseas.

Rome's acquisition of an empire was surprisingly haphazard. Rivalry with the other international power of the day, the North African merchant state of Carthage, involved the city in three wars, lasting on and off for more than a century from 264 to 146 BC. During the course of these wars, Rome acquired total control over – or at the very least considerable influence in – Sicily, Sardinia, Corsica, Spain, northern Africa, Egypt and Asia Minor.

A direct result of this military success was the growing power of a professional army under a series of talented and ambitious commanders. In 49 BC Julius Caesar, who had already conquered most of Gaul and had launched an invasion of Britain, started a civil war against those Romans, such as Pompey,

SENATVSPOPVLVSQVEROMANVS
IMPCAESARIDIVINERVAEFNERVAE
TRAIANOAVGGERMDACICOPONTIF
MAXIMOTRIBPOTXVIIIMPVICOSVIPP
ADDECLARANDVMQVANTAEALTITVDINIS
MONSETLOCVSTANT̄̄̄̄̄̄̄̄̄̄IBVSSITEGESTVS

CLASSIC CHARACTERS The inscription on the base of Trajan's Column in Rome mentions the amount of earth shifted to build the monument; the characters themselves have inspired stone carvers and typographers through the ages.

who upheld the rule of the Senate. In 44 BC he had himself appointed dictator for life, thus effectively bringing to an end, after almost 500 years, the government of the Roman Republic.

From then on, the influence of the Senate, which had previously been supposed to wield power in the interests of the people, went into decline. Despite cosmetic attempts to preserve the appearance of constitutional legitimacy, Julius Caesar's great-nephew Octavian (who became emperor as Augustus in 27 BC) had absolute control, as did his successors. Shortly after Augustus's stepson Tiberius had succeeded him as emperor in

AD 14, the power to elect magistrates was removed from the people – and, from then on, many of them were nominated by the emperor himself.

THE SECRET OF SUCCESS

How was it that the inhabitants of a few farming villages, set in the hills above the mouth of the Tiber river, came to dominate the entire Mediterranean world for almost a thousand years? Part of the credit must go to the Roman character.

In the 1st century AD, satirists such as Juvenal and Martial liked to poke fun at their contemporaries, portraying them as good-for-nothing decadents. In fact, though, the Romans were for the most part an upright people: sober, energetic and frugal. This much is evident from the puritanism of the satirists themselves. Juvenal is always yearning for the 'good old days', comparing the contemporary immorality of Roman wives, for example, with the times 'when the humble position of Latium's women kept them chaste . . . their tiny cabins were saved from corruption by heavy work, short hours of sleep, and hands that were chafed and calloused by Tuscan wool'. The Romans particularly loved the

continued on page 12

LATIN LETTERS

The Latin alphabet (which was derived from the Greek) is the most widely used of all the alphabets in the world. It has been adopted in all those regions where the early Christian church had some impact: even in countries, such as Poland and the Czech Republic, which speak a Slavonic language, the Latin alphabet is used, rather than the Cyrillic writing system used in Russia.

ANTONINE WALL
Under Roman occupation
AD 80-120
HADRIAN'S WALL
c AD122

Eboracum

Aquae Arnemetiae
Deva
Lindum
Viroconium
Ratae
Venta
Icenorum

BRITANNIA

Glevum
Corinium
Verulamium
Camulodunum
Aquae Sulis
Londinium
Calleva
Durovernum
Venta Belgarum
Atrebatum
Noviomagus

50°

North
Sea

Eboracum

BRITANNIA

Londinium

Colonia
Agrippina

GERMANIA
(INFERIOR)

BELGICA
Augusta
Treverorum

Durocortorum

LUGDUNENSIS

Seine

Rhine

Danube

RHAETIA

NORICUM

Loire

Augustodunum

GERMANIA
(SUPERIOR)

Augusta
Rauricorum

PANN

AQUITANIA
Ledosus
Lugdunum

Burdigala
Condatomagus

The Alps

NARBONENSIS

Rhône

Po

VIA AEMILIA

ITALIA

Adriatic S

Arelate

Narbonensis

Baeterrae
Massilia
Forum Iulii

Pont du Gard

40°

Tarraco

CORSICA

VIA AURELIA

ROMA

Ostia

Segovia

TARRACONENSIS

Tiber

VIA APPIA

LUSITANIA

Alcantara

Tagus

Misenum

Mt Vesuvius

Emerita Augusta

SARDINIA

ATLANTIC

BAETICA

OCEAN

Hispalis

Carthago Nova

M e d i t e r

Caesarea

SICILIA

Syra

Carthago

MAURETANIA
TINGITANIA

MAURETANIA
CAESARIENSIS

Thamugadi

AFRICA
PROCONSULARIS

Thysdrus

30°

NUMIDIA

Atlas Mts

Gulf of Gabès

Leptis Mag

TRIPOLITANIA

1 ALPES GRAIAE
2 ALPES COTTIAE
3 ALPES MARITIMAE

Sahara

Roman acquisitions at the end of the 2nd Punic War, 201BC
Roman acquisitions up to the death of Caesar, 44BC
Roman acquisitions up to the death of Augustus, AD14
Roman acquisitions up to the death of Trajan, AD117
Provincial boundary
Fortified frontier
Road
Route of Hannibal, 218 – 216BC
Site of Battle

0   500 km
0   300 miles

BUILDING THE ROMAN EMPIRE

THE MAP shows major stages in the expansion of Rome. Italy and southern Spain became part of the Roman Empire by 201 BC; Gaul, northern Africa, Greece and parts of Asia Minor by 44 BC; Egypt and eastern Europe to the Danube by AD 14; and Britain, Romania and more of Asia Minor by AD 117.

MODERN NAMES OF SOME MAJOR PLACES:

Aelia Capitolina	Jerusalem	Calleva Atrebatum	Silchester
Ancyra	Ankara	Camulodunum	Colchester
Aquae Arnemetiae	Buxton	Carthago	Carthage
Aquae Sulis	Bath	Carthago Nova	Cartagena
Arelate	Arles	Colonia Agrippina	Köln
Athenae	Athens	Condatomagus	Graufesenque
Augusta Rauricorum	Augst	Corinium	Cirencester
Augusta Treverorum	Trier	Deva	Chester
Augustodunum	Autun	Durocortorum	Reims
Baeterrae	Béziers	Durovernum	Canterbury
Burdigala	Bordeaux	Eboracum	York
Byzantium	Istanbul	Emerita Augusta	Mérida
Caesarea	Cherchel	Forum Iulii	Fréjus
		Glevum	Gloucester
		Hispalis	Seville

Ledosus	Lezoux
Lindum	Lincoln
Lugdunum	Lyons
Massilia	Marseilles
Noviomagus	Chichester
Pergamum	Bergama
Ratae	Leicester
Roma	Rome
Thamugadi	Timgad
Thessalonica	Thessaloniki
Thysdrus	El Djem
Trapezus	Trabzon
Venta Belgarum	Winchester
Verulamium	St Albans
Viroconium	Wroxeter

story of Cincinnatus, who had been approached by a delegation of senators as he ploughed his fields in 458 BC, had been elected dictator, and then won a crucial victory – all within the space of 16 days – before returning to his farm to continue his simple existence. In his praise of just such a simple life, Juvenal claimed that 'the less we indulge our pleasures the more we enjoy them'; to accuse someone of being a slave to his passions was one of the worst insults a Roman could level.

In ancient Rome, there was almost no distinction between public and private life. Everyone knew what was going on in the streets where most people spent most of their time. Even in the crowded homes there was very little privacy. Perhaps as a result of this, the Romans were rarely troubled by introspection, and their formidable energies were directed towards practical and public endeavours.

They were also deeply competitive. They did not hesitate to censure each other's behaviour in public, particularly if it did not conform to normal practice. The rich frantically sought public office, loudly advertising their personal generosity in providing public buildings and entertainments. In no sphere of activity did this desire for personal glory coincide more closely with the Romans' patriotic devotion than in their search for military victory.

The result was that Rome was an intensely militaristic society, where warlike skills and success were highly rewarded with fame, in the form of triumphal processions and political advancement, and fortune, in the form of booty and the rights of a conquering general and his followers to exploit a new province economically. As a result, the city often went to war to satisfy the ambitions of her competitive generals, rather than as part of an overall imperial strategy.

THE ART OF GOVERNMENT

Roman society was dynamic because the drive and determination of its citizens were channelled by personal competition into public projects, particularly military ones. This was how they acquired an empire. But they kept one through their pragmatic methods of government and their adaptability.

In the early days, the Romans had exacted tribute from their subject Italian peoples in the form of soldiers, who then conquered more territories on Rome's behalf. Later, the Romans encouraged their conquered peoples to govern themselves, so long as they paid their taxes and maintained law and order. Up to a point, then, the empire ran itself.

As the empire grew, it became increasingly cosmopolitan, for as well as introducing its own customs to other people, Rome was influenced, in turn, by the people it came to dominate – particularly the Greeks. In the words of the poet Horace, who like some other wealthy Romans had been educated partly in Athens: 'Captive Greece made captive her rude conqueror.' Juvenal was less happy with the development: 'There is one race of men which the very wealthiest among us find highly acceptable socially, but which I find particularly repulsive. About this race I am eager to speak, and no artificial sense of decorum will silence me. Citizens, I cannot bear a Rome that has become a Greek city. And yet, what portion of the dregs in our city is Greek?' Despite such xenophobia, the cosmopolitan character of Rome was a revitalising strength rather than a weakness, and one which was to influence many aspects of life in later centuries.

THE LEGACY OF ROME

The Roman peace, or *Pax Romana*, was the longest period of unification the Western world – including the territory of what are now some 30 different sovereign states – has ever known. Its effects reached into many areas of life and were often long-lasting. In law, for instance, it took a world previously based on a haphazard mix of tribal customs and replaced it with one founded on written laws. These came from Rome's own legal code, first written down in the 5th century BC in a form known as the Twelve Tables, although they were not properly recodified until the reign of the emperor Justinian in the 6th century AD. Many of the code's principles – particularly its emphasis on the spirit as well as the letter of the law – are still fundamental to the practice of the law.

When it came to the arts, the Romans themselves acknowledged that they were overshadowed by the ancient Greeks. Nevertheless, one of the fields in which they were genuinely inventive was architecture. Their designs and techniques, such as the development of the round arch and the vault, have continued to influence the buildings of

ARCHITECTURAL INFLUENCE Roman temples, such as the Maison Carrée at Nîmes in France, were influenced partly by Etruscan architecture (the raised platform on which they stood) and partly by Greek (the columns).

POETIC INSPIRATION In a mosaic from a Tunisian villa, the poet Virgil holds a scroll from his epic, the *Aeneid;* he is flanked by two Muses.

most revolutionary and influential of all was the great dome of Rome's Pantheon. This became the inspiration for two of the world's finest buildings: the church of Hagia Sophia which was built in the 6th century AD in Constantinople (now Istanbul), and the Church of St Peter in Rome.

Roman writers have been equally influential. The satires of Horace and Juvenal, the epigrams of Martial, and the pastoral *Eclogues* of Virgil have all been models for countless later generations of poets, while Virgil's *Aeneid*, the story of the wanderings of Aeneas from the fall of Troy to the founding of Rome, carried on the epic tradition of the Greek poet Homer. In a rather drier fashion, the Romans' emphasis on the teaching of rhetoric survived until the early 19th century – with the writings and speeches of the orator Cicero (106-43 BC) serving as required reading for generations of schoolboys.

The Latin language, meanwhile, made its mark from the start. With the exception of some Greek-speaking cities, the subjects of Rome generally welcomed the language of their conquerors and gradually abandoned their native tongues – Etruscan or Ligurian in Italy, Celtic in Britain, Iberian in Spain, and so on. In some countries, such as Germany and Britain, later invaders introduced Germanic and Slavonic tongues which displaced Latin. But its influence on French, Spanish, Italian and Romanian is still particularly evident in their everyday vocabulary. Bread, for example, is *panis* in Latin, *pain* in French, *pane* in Italian, *pan* in Spanish and *pîne* in Romanian. Even though English is basically a Germanic language, one word in four comes from Latin. Some of these words are direct survivors from Roman Britain; many others arrived indirectly via French words introduced by the Normans in the 11th century.

the Western world to the present day. Ever since, the Renaissance architects, from the Italian Andrea Palladio in the 16th century to the Scotsman Robert Adam in the 18th century and the Englishman Sir Edwin Lutyens in the 20th, have been rediscovering the architecture of ancient Rome. Much of this they have learnt through the writings of the Roman architect Marcus Vitruvius Pollio (*c.*90-20 BC), which described city plans and the layout of public and private buildings. But another source of inspiration has been the survival of the types of building that would have been found in any Roman town.

The basilica, for example, which served as the usual design for law courts, was rectangular in shape, with aisles on either side flanked by columns. It survived as the basic design for Christian churches for more than a thousand years. A Roman temple – the Maison Carrée at Nîmes in France – inspired the American statesman and amateur architect Thomas Jefferson in his design for the State Capitol at Richmond, Virginia (1785). Perhaps

LIFE IN THE ROMAN FAMILY

Painted on the wall of a house in Pompeii, this couple peer pensively at us across the gulf of almost 2000 years. The toga that the man is wearing is a symbol of his citizenship, and the stylus and writing tablet held by the woman are a sign of her education: advantages that the couple wanted made known. Ancient Rome was a status-conscious society, and nowhere was this more true than in the family, where every member – man, woman and child – knew their place.

MEN, WOMEN AND MARRIAGE

Wedding rings, an early form of confetti, and the custom of carrying

the bride over the threshold are all Roman traditions recognisable today.

So too are the rights that were increasingly enjoyed by the women of imperial Rome.

THE SANCTITY OF THE FAMILY was one of the cornerstones of Roman society, but the Romans had a somewhat different understanding of the term 'family' from ours. Unlike the small family unit of today, where all the members tend to have a say, the Roman *paterfamilias*, the father and head of the family, was traditionally all-powerful, ruling the lives of his extended household with a rod of iron, from his wife, children and foster-children down to his slaves. In the early days of Rome, at least, the paterfamilias had the power of life and death over his children; and even until the 3rd century AD he could, if he chose, legally abandon a newborn child on a lonely hillside or public refuse tip to be adopted by strangers or to perish from cold and hunger.

In ancient Rome, most people married for practical rather than romantic reasons. 'Women are married for the sake of bearing children and heirs, and not for pleasure and enjoyment', wrote Soranus, the best known writer on obstetrics and gynaecology in the ancient world. Men, too, wanted sons and heirs. They also wanted the dowry (around a million sesterces for a wealthy family, as well as farms, apartment blocks and slaves), although the stated purpose of this was to help the husband maintain the wife during marriage. As a result, competition for fertile and wealthy brides was intense. Many women moved from husband to husband, even while pregnant, in a kind of marital merry-go-round: there are even instances of wives returning – with their dowries – to their original husbands after several marriages in between. Under these circumstances, the power of the husband over his wife gradually weakened, through custom and changes in the law, until a form of marriage developed that was not dissimilar to our own.

By the 1st century BC, the form of marriage in which the wife formally came under the authority of her husband had mostly given way to a form of marriage known as *sine manu* – without authority. A wife kept her original family name when she got married and remained under the formal authority of her father

STATUESQUE **A young Roman woman wears a cloak draped loosely over a long tunic.**

EYEWITNESS

'SHE LOVED HER HUSBAND WITH ALL HER HEART'

THE EPITAPHS on tombstones were addressed to passers-by. One from the 2nd century BC describes the qualities of a dutiful Roman wife: ❧ Stranger, I have only a few words to say. Stop and read them. – This is the unlovely tomb of a lovely woman. Her parents named her Claudia. She loved her husband with all her heart. She bore two sons; one of these she leaves here on earth, the other she has already placed under the earth. She was charming in speech, yet pleasant and proper in manner. She managed the household well. She spun wool. – I have spoken. Go on your way. ❧

PEN PORTRAIT **A young woman uses a bone stylus to write on a wooden tablet coated on one side with wax.**

rather than her husband. She had her own share of power in the household, running the home, controlling its finances, particularly when the husband was away on business or military service, and supervising the upbringing of her children until they started at school. She also had a certain amount of financial and personal freedom, making her own will, dining at table with her husband and guests, and walking to the baths and public games, perhaps with a companion. You only have to look at the riotous – if exceptional – lifestyle of ladies such as Clodia, the mistress of the poet Catullus, in the 1st century AD, or of empresses such as Messalina to realise that the woman's lot had changed considerably since the days when the wife was placed under her husband's control.

In law, the cohabitation of a freed or freeborn couple – along with some stated intention of togetherness – constituted marriage. There was no need for any written document (apart, perhaps, from a contract for the bride's dowry) and no need for any official sanction. Nevertheless, many people went in for more formal ceremonies, which were usually paid for by the bride's father. The marriages of most wealthy Roman citizens were arranged, with a view to their dynastic and financial advantage, by members of the family. The couple might be betrothed first – an event sometimes symbolised by the gift of a ring – before marrying at the age of 14 or 15 for girls, and between five and ten years older for boys.

MOTHER AND CHILD **Messalina, wife of the emperor Claudius holds her son Britannicus.**

On the day of the wedding – the second half of June was considered particularly auspicious – the female relatives of the bride dressed her in a belted white tunic and a saffron-coloured cloak, arranged her hair in six plaits held together by ribbons, and placed a bright flame-coloured veil over her head and orange slippers on her feet.

THE ROMAN WEDDING

When the groom arrived at his bride's father's house, a pig was sacrificed to the gods, and its entrails checked for omens. Once the groom had taken his bride's right hand in his, and the couple had exchanged vows of fidelity, there was a banquet to celebrate the alliance of the two families. As this drew to a close, the groom – in an act of ritual abduction – pretended to steal his bride from her mother's arms and took her off to his own parents' home, accompanied by a procession of flute-players, torchbearers and guests, singing, scattering nuts like confetti among the crowd in the street, and shouting dirty jokes as protection against the 'evil eye' (the abuse made the couple appear less

ANCIENT WEDDING RINGS

The modern practice of wearing a wedding ring dates back at least to Roman times when, in some engagement ceremonies, the bride slipped a ring onto the third finger of her left hand. According to the philosopher Aulus Gellius, anatomists had shown that a 'delicate nerve' led from what he termed the 'annular finger' to the heart.

fortunate and therefore less attractive to evil spirits). On arrival at her in-laws' home, the bride put down the spindle and distaff she had been carrying as symbols of her new matronly responsibility and smeared the door with oil and strands of wool before being carried over the threshold by her attendants. The next day, there was another party – this time at her in-laws' house – at which the new bride worshipped at the altar of her husband's family. Generally, the new couple would then begin their married life here.

WIFELY DUTIES

The Roman wife was supposed to devote herself to household tasks, such as spinning and weaving, which were held to embody the traditional virtues. The ideal Roman wife was kind, compliant, faithful and fertile, like a woman called Amymone during the emperor Hadrian's reign, whose virtues were catalogued as 'very good and very beautiful, a woolmaker, pious, righteous, thrifty, chaste, staying at home'. And women who tried to break the rules were disparaged.

Despite the claims of 1st-century moralists and 20th-century moralisers that family life – and therefore the fabric of society – began to crumble under the Empire, there is no reason to believe that Roman marriages were any more or less happy than many others in history. There are

RING OF DEVOTION **Married couples exchanged rings, such as this one showing a pair of clasped hands.**

WEDDING PROCESSION Accompanied by well-wishers, a groom leads his bride to his family home.

'A JUST RETURN FOR A BRIDE'S VIRGINITY'

MARRIAGES were usually arranged by family members. Here is a letter dating from the 1st century AD from Pliny the Younger to a friend, Junius Mauricius, who is hoping to arrange a marriage for his niece:

❦ You ask me to look out for a husband for your brother's daughter, a responsibility which I feel is very rightly mine; for you know how I have always loved and admired him as the finest of men. . . .

I should have had a long search if Minicius Acilianus were not at hand, as if he were made for us. He loves me as warmly as one young man does another (he is a little younger than I am), but respects me as his elder, for he aspires to be influenced and guided by me, as I was by you and your brother. His native place is Brixia, one of the towns in our part of Italy which still retains intact much of its honest simplicity along with the rustic virtues of the past. His father is Minicius Macrinus, who chose to remain a leading member of the order of knights because he desired nothing higher . . . His maternal grandmother, Serrana Procula, comes from the town of Patavium, whose reputation you know; but Serrana is a model of propriety even to Patavians. His uncle, Publius Acilius, is a man of exceptional character, wisdom and integrity. You will in fact find nothing to criticise in the whole household, any more than in your own.

Acilianus himself has abundant energy and application, but no lack of modesty. He has held the offices of quaestor, tribune and praetor with great distinction, thus sparing you the necessity of canvassing on his behalf. He has a frank expression, and his complexion is fresh and high-coloured; his general good looks have a natural nobility and the dignified bearing of a senator. (I think these points should be mentioned, as a sort of just return for a bride's virginity.) . . . ❦

many instances in classical literature of obvious affection between spouses, such as that of Pliny the Younger for his third wife, the much younger Calpurnia: 'I stay awake most of the night thinking of you,' he wrote while they were apart, 'and by day I find my feet carrying me . . . to your room at the times I usually visited you; then finding it empty I depart, as sick and sorrowful as a lover locked out.'

However, what did become a matter of official concern during the Empire was the number of childless marriages. Because of the dangers of childbirth (and according to some men, because of the damage done to their wives' figures), many women were wary of having children and resorted to some fairly rudimentary forms of contraception.

BIRTH CONTROLS

These included abstinence, magic charms and the insertion of pepper, olive oil, honey, the sap from a tree, sponges or plugs of wool into the mouth of the uterus. Most radical of all, Pliny even suggested that the surest form of birth control was to depress desire all together, for example by smearing mouse dung on parts of the body.

Although Soranus recognised that 'it is safer to

**FUNERARY RELIEF
A Roman couple, attended by their dog, engage in conversation: a depiction, after death, of their happy years together.**

SHOPKEEPER Many Roman women worked for a living, such as this one working in a poulterer's shop.

prevent conception from occurring than to destroy the foetus through abortion', wealthy women also induced termination through violent exercise or drugs. 'It's rare for a gilded bed to contain a woman in labour,' complained the poet Juvenal, 'so efficacious now are the drugs and skills of the female who renders women sterile, and is paid for murdering people within the womb.'

Many theories have been suggested for the Romans' relative childlessness, including their liking for long, hot baths and alcohol, both of which tend to reduce male fertility. But the most compelling explanation is that most Roman women died before the age of 30 – thereby limiting their childbearing years. Given that many Roman mothers breastfed

CAMEO ROLE
A pendant bears the profiles of Emperor Claudius (left) with his wife Agrippina the Younger, and the Roman general Germanicus (right) with Agrippina the Elder.

their children for up to three years, during which time their chances of conceiving were reduced, and given the long absence of Republican husbands on military campaigns or on tours of administrative duty in the provinces, it was unusual for even the most fertile women to have more than four or five children. Death in childbirth (which killed more women than the number of men killed in battle) would account for many mothers; and infant mortality for many children – as would epidemics, such as smallpox, dysentery or even measles, which regularly swept the city.

As only 50 per cent of children reached puberty, a couple had to have at least four children if two of them were to reach an age where they could become parents themselves and maintain a stable population. Augustus's attempts to stem the decline in the birthrate included rewards, such as tax exemptions for couples who had three children or more, and laws that forced widows to remarry within two years of their husband's

EYEWITNESS

'THESE LITTLE TOUCHES WIN OVER SIMPLE FEMALE HEARTS'

IN 'THE ART OF LOVE', the poet Ovid gives his readers some advice on how to conduct an affair at the races. The emperor Augustus exiled Ovid to a town on the Black Sea coast, possibly for encouraging adultery in this way.

❛ Don't neglect the horse races if you're looking for a place to meet your girlfriend. A circus crowded with people offers many advantages. You don't have to use a secret sign language here or be content with a slight nod to acknowledge one another's presence. Sit right next to your girlfriend – no one will stop you – and squeeze up beside her as closely as possible. It's really easy to do. The narrowness of each seating space forces you to squeeze together; in fact the rules for seating compel you to touch her!

Conversation should begin with no problem; just start out with the same comments that everyone else is making. Be sure to ask with great interest which horses are running and then immediately cheer for the same one, whichever it is, that she cheers for.

Perhaps a speck of dust will settle on your girlfriend's breast (it often happens); be sure to brush it off with your hand. Even if there is no speck of dust, pretend – and keep brushing off nothing! Take advantage of every opportunity. If her skirt is trailing too far along the ground, pick up the edge of it and carefully lift the soiled part off the dust. At once you'll receive a reward for your careful concern; you'll be able to look at her legs, and she won't mind.

In addition, turn to whoever is sitting behind her and ask him not to jab her in the back with his knees. These little touches win over simple female hearts. Many men have found it useful to bring along a cushion which they can offer. It's also helpful to fan her with the racing programme and to give her a stool for her dainty feet. Yes, the circus provides many opportunities for initiating a love affair. ❜

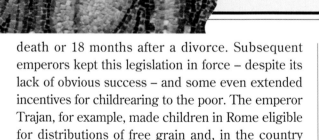

ART OF LOVE
A pair of lovers embrace in this mosaic dating from the 4th century AD.

death or 18 months after a divorce. Subsequent emperors kept this legislation in force – despite its lack of obvious success – and some even extended incentives for childrearing to the poor. The emperor Trajan, for example, made children in Rome eligible for distributions of free grain and, in the country towns of Italy, organised an endowment scheme to support local children. None of these measures, however, halted the inevitable decline in the citizen population, and new members had to be recruited from outside: foreigners and enfranchised slaves.

THE BREAK-UP OF A MARRIAGE

In the austere days of the Republic, a man's adultery was left unpunished, whereas adultery by a woman was considered punishable by death; indeed, some of the women involved in the Bacchanalian scandal of 186 BC were privately executed by their own families. Despite such sanctions (which became less draconian with time), adultery was commonplace by the 1st century AD. Many wealthier citizens took what pleasures they could from female slaves in their own households, fathering children who

DID YOU KNOW?

So rare was it for women not to marry that there was no Latin word for 'spinster' – the word for 'widow' covered all women without a husband. Aristocratic women in imperial Rome had legal rights to own, inherit and bequeath property that were not surpassed – in Britain, at least – until the Married Woman's Property Act of 1870.

ATTENTION SEEKING A small child, thought to be Augustus's grandson, tries to attract the attention of his parents in this detail from the Altar of Augustan Peace.

whom. But they led to some strange anomalies: until a loophole in the law was changed, some otherwise respectable women registered as prostitutes in order legally to continue their affairs with freeborn men.

Getting a divorce was easy, and the breakup of a marriage was often prompted by exactly the same political or financial reasons that had encouraged it in the first place. In the 2nd century BC, the grounds for divorce could be as flimsy and one-sided as a husband objecting to his wife going out without a veil or attending the games without his permission – as well as more serious grounds, such as adultery. In the 1st century BC, the Roman leader Sulla even divorced his third wife for infertility. Over the centuries, however, divorce stopped being solely the man's prerogative and could be initiated by either husband or wife, or even by either partner's paterfamilias. All that either party had to do was to announce their intention of divorcing, possibly by letter or messenger; under Augustus's divorce laws, it was also necessary for the divorcing party to issue a public statement of intent in front of seven witnesses.

In general, the father kept custody of the children after the divorce, and they would be brought up in his household. The only time that the law became involved was to settle the disposition of property. As time went by, the old tradition – in which the husband retained control of his wife's dowry – lapsed, and it became the custom to return it to the wife's father after the divorce, unless the wife had been found guilty of committing adultery; if this was the case, a proportion of her dowry was retained by her husband.

might be brought up alongside, if not equally with, the legitimate children of the household. This was considered perfectly acceptable and legal behaviour, as was a visit to a prostitute. But many citizens also embarked on affairs with women of their own class; and this was not considered acceptable.

DIVORCE LAWS
The emperor Augustus, who was himself married three times and had not hesitated from divorcing his second wife Scribonia and stealing Livia Drusilla, who was six months pregnant at the time, from her husband, passed laws punishing adultery for both men and women. One of these forced the husband to divorce his wife if she was caught in the act of adultery. Laws such as this to curb extramarital affairs between free men and women stemmed less from a moral perspective than from a desire to protect the legitimacy of upper-class family descent: so that everyone knew exactly who was the legitimate heir of

DOUBLE PORTRAIT
This funerary monument, dating from the end of the 1st century BC, shows a couple from the freedman class.

23

TOMBS AND EPITAPHS

Funeral art and inscriptions reveal much about the Roman

attitude to death, but even more about their everyday lives.

GROWING UP A panel from the sarcophagus of a dead child shows the boy's progression from babyhood, through playing at driving a cart, to doing his homework in rhetoric at his father's house.

AT FESTIVALS, such as the Parentalia, the feast of the dead which lasted from February 13 to February 21 each year, the ancient Romans visited their family tombs with offerings of flowers, bread, salt, milk and wine for loved ones who had passed away. This tradition stemmed from the Roman belief that the grave was home on earth for the dead. People were often buried with their personal effects – cups, lamps, jewellery, or small toy figurines in the case of children – to reassure them in the afterlife.

During the 2nd century AD, more and more people were buried rather than cremated. The poorest might be bundled into the ground in a sack; richer people were laid to rest in a coffin made of wood or stone, with a lead lining, and the wealthiest of all might be placed in a magnificent marble sarcophagus and deposited in a family vault.

The grave was generally marked by a tombstone. Some were made of wood. Most of those that have survived were made of stone and bear an inscription, giving details of the person's name, rank, occupation and age, and the name of the person who had erected the monument. The inscription usually ends with a dedication in Latin, meaning 'To the Spirits of the departed'.

There might also be a bust, a statue or a carved relief of the deceased. Portraits were not necessarily that true to life, however, since stonemasons produced stocks of ready-made monuments: a businessman poring over his accounts, a shopkeeper surrounded by the tools of his trade, a general accepting the surrender of a barbarian chief, and so on. Alternatively, they might promote the personal qualities of the deceased: a man reading a book to signify learning, or a woman burning an offering of incense to the gods to denote piety.

PET CARE On her tombstone, a young girl clutches her kitten – one of the earliest European depictions of the cat as a pet.

MILLER'S MONUMENT On the tomb of a wealthy miller, a donkey (on the left) is used to drive a quernstone for grinding flour; on the right are sieves and barrels for storing the flour.

UNDER THE VOLCANO As at Pompeii, cemeteries were generally sited just beyond the town walls.

Archaeologists have recorded some 100 000 Roman epitaphs, mostly from the 1st century AD. Many of these make a public point, claiming for example that the deceased 'worked hard'. Others deliver a reproach: a father disinheriting a daughter, say, or a mother accusing another woman of poisoning her son.

But as well as providing historians with a mass of statistical information, tombs and epitaphs give us a glimpse of the sorrows of people living almost 2000 years ago. A tombstone found near York mourns the death of a much-loved daughter, Corellia, who had died at the age of 13: 'You mysterious spirits of the deceased . . . who are sought by the paltry ashes and by the shade, the phantom of the body, after the brief light of life: I, the father of an innocent daughter, a pitiable victim of unfair hope, lament this, her final end.'

For reasons of hygiene, Roman law forbade burials within towns, and so cemeteries were generally established just outside the city gates. The roads out of Rome, Ostia, Pompeii and Herculaneum are all lined with graves keeping each other company against the loneliness of death. It was a great consolation to the living that, when they were dead, their tombs would catch the eye of a casual passer-by who would then linger on to read their epitaph: 'Read, passing friend,' runs a typical inscription, 'what role I played in the world . . . And now that you have read, have a pleasant journey.'

BUILDING ON A MONUMENTAL SCALE The tomb of the Haterii celebrates the family building business.

THE RAISING OF CHILDREN

Roman ideas about raising and educating children were based on the

notion that the child was, in words attributed to Emperor Augustus,

'a physical and mental mirror of yourself'.

MUCH OF WHAT IS KNOWN about Roman practices during pregnancy and childbirth comes from the writings of the eminent physician Soranus of Ephesus, who lived in Rome during the 2nd century AD. His *Gynaecology* provides a lot of commonsense advice that would not be out of place in a modern manual on pregnancy. He was aware of the nausea that often accompanies the early months and recommends the taking of gentle exercise and a balanced diet – although 'one must not pay attention to the popular saying that it is necessary to provide food as for two organisms'.

Most women gave birth at home, with the help of a midwife if not a physician. The woman sat in a birthing chair, gripping the arms, while the midwife squatted in front easing the delivery. It was a dangerous business, and as many as one in forty women died in childbirth or in complications arising from it.

As soon as a child was born, it was placed on the ground at the feet of the father, who would then decide whether to accept it as a member of the family. If the child was deformed or, particularly in poorer families, if it was a girl and was therefore considered too expensive a future burden in terms of food, clothing and a dowry, the father might decide to 'expose' the child. Quite simply, the poor little bundle would be abandoned in the street or, as recent excavations have shown, buried beneath the floors of a house or in the foundations of a new building. On the other hand, if the father decided to recognise the child, he would assume responsibility for it and rights over it. The parents might then celebrate the happy event by painting the announcement of the birth on the wall of the house.

LUCKY CHARM   A newborn child was given a *bulla* to ward off evil spirits, like this gold one found in Pompeii.

The child would then be fed by the mother or a wet nurse, usually a slave (Soranus favoured maternal breast-feeding), and placed in swaddling clothes – a first taste of the tough regime that was to come. Bands were tied around the baby's ankles, knees, hips, elbows and wrists, and splints were attached to its legs to keep them straight and to mould the body. Eight days after the birth of a girl and nine of a boy, the child was named and given a *bulla* – a good-luck charm to ward off evil spirits. Children were weaned at the age of two or three.

About one in three Roman children died within the first year (as opposed to around one in a hundred in most industrialised countries today and one in five in many Third World countries). Many babies fell prey to diarrhoea and dysentery – particularly if they had been fed on non-sterile cow's or goat's milk, rather than breast milk. It is small wonder that there were so many recommendations for ways of looking after infants: for instance, in the 2nd century BC, Cato advised bathing babies in urine passed by someone who had eaten cabbage, and in the 1st century AD, Pliny the Elder's remedy for infant diarrhoea was to smear the wet-nurse's or mother's breast with hare's rennet.

It has been argued by some sociologists

WRAP UP   A stone relief of a baby clothed in swaddling bands.

that because of such high infant mortality, Roman parents were wary of making too much of an emotional investment in their children: that they were cold and uncaring. And it is certainly true that there is little literary evidence of that sense of delight and affection so typical of 20th-century writings about parenthood. Yet the Romans did care passionately about their children, for they represented a massive investment in the future. The state needed soldiers to fight in the legions; poor parents expected their children to look after them in old age; and wealthy parents needed successors to maintain the family name and honour.

In the absence of suitable sons, however, Romans were happy to adopt the children of other people as their heirs and successors; indeed, several of the Roman emperors of the 1st and 2nd centuries AD were succeeded by adopted sons, in much the same way as Julius Caesar was succeeded by Augustus.

AN UNSENTIMENTAL EDUCATION

Education started at home, with the learning of letters and simple reading. These skills would be essential in later life, since Rome – for the upper classes at least – was a literate society with written calendars, registers and regulations playing a great part in public life, and contracts, accounts and ancient family remedies most important in private life.

Education was traditionally the responsibility of the father, and one which some men such as the Republican politician Cato the Elder, who taught his son reading, writing, horse-riding and swimming himself, took very seriously. Other wealthy parents, however, delegated the duty to a slave, who acted as tutor or

BIRTH DAY In this terracotta relief from the port of Ostia, a midwife helps a mother, who is seated in a birthing chair, to deliver her child.

childminder and was known as a *paedagogus*, from which comes our word 'pedagogue'. (Many pedagogues, whose duties included escorting the child to school when they were the right age, were Greek – a race much respected by the Romans for their learning.)

At the age of seven, boys from the poorest families might start work in the fields or learn a craft; boys from richer families might continue their education at home or go to a fee-paying elementary school, the *ludus litterarius*. But whether at home or in school, primary studies were limited to reading, writing and arithmetic (essentially addition and subtraction on an abacus).

Roman writing consisted of a string of words without punctuation, which the reader had to decipher as best he could by mumbling them to himself to make any sense. So the child's first task was to learn each of the letters of the alphabet by rote, to repeat words and phrases as the master read them from the text, and then to copy ancient maxims by scratching them onto a

FAMILY OUTING At official ceremonies, such as this procession of the imperial family, children often dressed like their parents.

TELLING THE TIME IN ANCIENT ROME

TIMEKEEPING in ancient Rome was a rather imprecise art. In the early days, the Romans simply divided the day into two halves: morning and afternoon, which an official would announce when the sun passed between two monuments in the Forum. However, in the 3rd century BC, one of the consuls brought a Greek sundial back from Sicily. This was used for the next 100 years or so, regardless of the fact that its height, which determined the length of its shadow and therefore the reading of the time, was designed for a latitude different from Rome's. It was not until 164 BC that the Romans installed in the city a sundial designed for their own latitude. Other sundials ranged in size from tiny pocket versions to the monumental Egyptian obelisk that the emperor Augustus brought back from Egypt in 10 BC and installed in the Campus Martius (it is now in the Piazza di Montecitorio). The introduction of water clocks made it possible to tell the time at night, or when the weather was bad. Nevertheless, sundials and water clocks often disagreed; as Seneca complained, 'it was easier to get the philosophers to agree than the clocks'. More fundamental was the fact that the duration of an hour changed with the seasons. In Rome, the relative proportions of the daylight hours devoted to a particular activity remained the same, irrespective of the season. Work stopped in the middle of the afternoon – around 2.15 pm in winter and 3.45 pm in summer. In

TIMEPIECE Throughout the Empire, the Romans relied on sundials for telling the time, such as this one from Bulla Regia in Tunisia.

midwinter, when there were only about nine hours of daylight, each hour lasted around 45 minutes; and in midsummer, when there were just over 15 hours, each hour lasted about an hour and a quarter.

ANCIENT CLOCK The sundial on this pillar in Pompeii survived the eruption of Vesuvius in AD 79 largely intact.

CLASS TIME A school class spills out onto the
street, under the shade of a colonnade.

piece of pottery or by inscribing them onto a wax-
coated wooden tablet with a bone or bronze stylus.
In his *Confessions*, St Augustine recalled the un-
remitting monotony of school lessons in the 4th
century AD: '*unum et unum, duo*; *duo et duo, quat-
tuor . . .*' (one and one, two; two and two, four).

Most of these schools consisted of little more
than a single room – or, to avoid paying rent, the
teacher might take classes outside in the street,
holding them under a shop-awning or beneath the
portico of a rented apartment block, separated
from the bustle and noise of the crowd only by a
sheet of cloth. For the schoolteacher to scratch
even the most basic living classes had to be large

(he received only 50 denarii a month per pupil; the
average craftsman's salary was 50 denarii a day).
Nevertheless, the parents' expectations were high:
as Juvenal described in one of his satires: 'The
teacher's grammar has to be faultless; he must
read the stories in books, and know each one of
the writers like the back of his hand . . . Make sure
that he moulds the children's characters, just as a
sculptor models a face from wax with his thumb.
Make sure that in fact he's a father to the group. . . .'
Just like the father at home, the teacher did not
spare the rod, the leather thong or the eel-skin
strap; and it is no coincidence that the Latin teaching, *disciplina*, also means 'punishment'.

'TO BE KEPT AWAKE IS A SERIOUS VEXATION'

AMONG many other laments about metropolitan life, the poet Martial complained how the noise of school classes woke him up in the morning: ❧ What do you have against us, spiteful schoolteacher? We know you are hated by all the boys and girls you teach. Before the crested rooster has even crowed, you shatter the silence with your harsh voice and with lashes of your whip. The noises you make ring out as loudly as bronze beaten on an anvil when a metal sculptor is fashioning a lawyer mounted on a horse. Shouts in the Colosseum, when the crowd is cheering on its favourite gladiator, are not so deafening as your thunderous voice. Now we neighbours are not demanding that we be allowed to sleep without disturbance for the whole night; to be awakened briefly is a minor irritation. But to be kept awake is a serious vexation. So send your students home. Would you be willing, you old windbag, to accept the same pay for being silent as you now receive for shouting out lessons? ❧

Classes began at dawn and generally continued until noon or early afternoon. After school, pupils might go on to the public baths or play games with hoops, balls, knucklebones and nuts which they rolled like marbles. They also enjoyed leapfrog and blindman's buff, and acting games such as soldiers, gladiators or horse-riding (using a broomstick). Dolls made from terracotta, rags or ivory (for the very wealthy) were particularly popular with girls. Before their wedding day, they would dedicate them to the goddess Venus, as a sign that their childhood had come to an end.

This was as much schooling as the majority got, but around the age of 11, wealthier children went on to learn, first of all, the rules of Greek and Latin grammar and then the art of rhetoric. Learning grammar was a very dry and dreary business. Pupils pored over texts by long-dead authors such as the Latin playwright Livius Andronicus or the Greek poet Homer, analysing and commenting on them line by line, and word by word. On the way, they picked up a smattering of astronomy, music, history, natural science and philosophy. The language they were studying was itself already out of date – nothing like that spoken in the streets.

Learning rhetoric, which children started around the age of 14, was not much better. It was hardly a practical preparation for the adult world, but it did help the child to acquire the eloquence and powers of public speaking expected of a citizen in public assemblies and the law courts. Students continued to analyse ancient texts, but at this stage they also learnt how to write and recite their own compositions. The most advanced form of this was a six-part speech debating a historical or hypothetical subject.

For example, a student might re-create the discussions the Spartans had when deciding whether to fight to the last against the Persians at Thermopylae. Or he might tackle an utterly artificial but supposedly controversial issue. For example, would you claim to be the owner of the treasure if you had agreed to buy a fisherman's entire catch and then it was discovered that the catch included an ingot of gold trapped in the net? The situations became more hypothetical and melodramatic, involving family vendettas, murders, rapes, pirates and poisoners.

PUTTING AWAY THESE CHILDISH THINGS

At about 16, when privileged Roman youths left school, they went through a ceremony to mark their coming of age. This preliminary step towards full citizenship was often held at the forum during the festival of Liberalia on March 17. Watched by family and friends, the boy of good family surrendered the good-luck charm, or *bulla*, he had been given nine days after birth and exchanged the purple-edged toga, or *toga praetexta*, of boyhood for the plain light brown toga, or *toga virilis*, of manhood. His name was registered in the census of citizens, making him eligible a year later for conscription (during the Republic) and for other forms of public service such as the law (during the Empire). The young man could now become a soldier, an orator, a lawyer or a priest.

During the later days of the Empire, some young men went on to university to study philosophy, jurisprudence or medicine. Girls, however, stopped their education at 12 or 13, when they began to learn to be good housewives; their marriage a couple of years later turned them into adults, just as the donning of the toga virilis had done for the boys.

THE ROMANS
AT HOME

In this relief from Trier in Germany, a maid inserts pins into the hair of her mistress,
who appraises the result in a polished metal mirror. Two more maids,
carrying flasks of scented oil, look on admiringly. It is an early morning scene that
must have been typical of wealthy households throughout the Roman Empire.
Whereas most people had to make do with relatively poor housing, food and clothes,
the rich aspired to ever-greater comfort and extravagance.

LIFE IN THE CITY

Life on the streets of the greatest metropolis in the ancient world was crowded,

chaotic and occasionally violent: no wonder the wealthy wanted to

escape to the peace and quiet of their secluded villas.

THE TRADITIONAL VIEW of ancient Rome is of a gleaming white, well-ordered city built by some of the classical world's greatest architects and engineers. The reality was far from that. The Roman capital was, in fact, a tangle of tall houses, graffiti-daubed walls and narrow streets, which twisted and turned. It was very easy to get lost in the labyrinth of alleyways, where the only landmarks were the public monuments and temples. Roads which led out of Rome, such as the Appian Way, linking the city with its Eastern empire, were more than five yards wide; and so were the city's main thoroughfares, the Via Nova and the Via Sacra. But most of Rome's roads were no more than muddy tracks where the citizens waded ankle-deep through the rubbish (despite the law that made it the duty of the owner of the property on the street frontage to keep it clean) and the sewage (despite the celebrated Roman drainage system). Passers-by had to get out of the way of soldiers,

scavenging dogs, or of slaves carrying wealthy employers in litters or sedan chairs; and dodge their way past the barbers' stalls, moneychangers' booths and school classes that spilled into the street.

From the composure they exhibit in their statues and their writings, the Romans themselves often appear cold, calm and collected. In fact, they were probably not much different from their descendants today in Rome or Naples. They were essentially a Mediterranean people living their lives in the street. There was never any privacy. If you were poor, a whole family might sleep in a single room in a rented apartment; whereas a rich family was constantly surrounded by family members and slaves. Ancient Rome's population of more than a million in the 1st century AD was crowded into an area of less than 8 sq miles (20 km²). It has been calculated that around 50 people lived on the fourth and fifth storeys of the *insula*, or 'island house', at the foot of the Capitol Hill, with only two or three

---

EYEWITNESS

'GO STRAIGHT DOWN AND YOU'LL SEE A TEMPLE'

SO DIFFICULT was it to find your way around ancient Rome that the subject became the source of some humour – as in this scene from the play *Adelphoe* by Terence, writing in the 2nd century BC.

❛ *Syrus*: You know that colonnade near the meat market, down that way?

Demea: Of course I do.

S: Go straight up the street past it. Then there's a turning going

downhill; go straight down and you'll see a temple on this side and next to it that alley –

D: Which one?

S: Where there's a big fig-tree.

D: I know.

S: Go on through it.

D: *(after some thought)* That alley hasn't got a way through.

S: So it hasn't. What a fool I am. My mistake. Go back to the colonnade. Yes, this is a much

shorter way and less chance of going wrong. Do you know Cratinus's house, that rich fellow's? *(rapidly)* Go past it, turn left, straight up the street, come to the temple of Diana, then turn right and before you come to the city gate just by the pond there's a small flour mill and a workshop opposite . . . That's where he is. ❜

SHOPPING MALL   Paving stones wind up the slopes of Trajan's market. This multistorey group of some 150 shops and stalls, built into a hillside in the centre of Rome, formed part of a massive building programme.

SHOP SIGN Monkeys on the counter and rabbits in hutches accompany the chickens on a poulterer's sign from Ostia.

square yards (1.6 or 2.5 m²) per person – little more than the space required to lie down in. It is no wonder that people spent so much of their spare time outside on the streets.

Rome's colonial cities were generally built from scratch on a piece of razed land at a crossroads. They were planned, rather like a military camp, around two main axes, the *cardo* which ran from north to south and the *decumanus* which ran from east to west. Off these principal thoroughfares led a grid of parallel streets. Rome, on the other hand, grew organically. What town planning there was was precipitated first by fires and then by the ambition of successive emperors to outdo the building programmes of their predecessors. Perhaps the most terrible fire of all was the one in AD 64 during Nero's reign, which spread rapidly through the flimsily built houses. It raged for six days and nights, and at the end, according to the historian Tacitus, only four of the city's regions 'remained

BUILDING WORK In a detail from a Pompeian fresco, a carpenter uses a hammer and chisel; there is a bow drill on the floor.

intact, while three were laid level with the ground. In the other seven, nothing survived but a few dilapidated and half-burned shells of houses.' It was only after the fire – and particularly in the 2nd century AD – that the city acquired a town plan and the emperors embarked on a massive programme of public building, of baths, circuses, palaces, granaries, markets, squares and a forest of columns and monumental arches.

THE ROMAN APARTMENT BLOCK

All over the city, opulent houses rubbed shoulders with humble terrace homes and workshops. From the 2nd century BC, more and more city dwellers

CROSSWORD PUZZLE

The ancient Pompeians loved puzzles. Here is one found drawn on a column in the city. It consists of a square made up of five letters that can be read from left to right or right to left, from top to bottom or vice versa, and means 'Arepo the ploughman holds the wheels carefully'.

```
R  O  T  A  S
O  P  E  R  A
T  E  N  E  T
A  R  E  P  O
S  A  T  O  R
```

'WHO BUT THE RICH GET ANY SLEEP IN ROME?'

IN HIS THIRD SATIRE, Juvenal describes how his friend Umbricius is leaving Rome for the calm of Cumae. As these extracts show, the reasons Umbricius gives for his departure include the ever-present risk of fire in the poorly built tenement blocks, the noise and the high levels of crime:

❛ Who at cool Praeneste or at Volsinii amid its leafy hills was ever afraid of his house falling down? Who in modest Gabii, or on the sloping heights of Tibur? But here [in Rome] we live in a city supported for the most part on slender props [scaffolding], for that is how the landlord holds up his tottering houses, patches up gaping cracks in the old walls and tells the inmates to sleep securely under a roof ready to fall around their ears. Ucalegon is below already shouting for water and moving his household goods: smoke is already pouring out of the third floor, but you know nothing of it, because if the alarm begins on the ground floor, the last to burn will be he who has nothing to protect him from the rain except the tiles, where the gentle doves lay their eggs.

What sleep is possible in a lodging? Who but the rich get any sleep in Rome? . . . The crossing of wagons in the narrow, winding streets, the cursing of the drivers when brought to a halt, would make sleep impossible even for the doziest of sea-cows – or Drusus. When the rich man has a social call to make, the mob makes way for him as he is carried aloft over their heads in his huge Liburnican litter. He writes or sleeps inside as he goes along, for the closed window

TRAFFIC RESTRICTION Because of the noise and chaos they caused, horse-drawn carriages were forbidden in Rome during the daytime from the time of Julius Caesar onwards.

induces slumber. Yet he will arrive before us; hurry as we may, we are blocked by a surging crowd in front, and by a dense mass of people pressing on us from behind: one man digs an elbow into me, another a hard sedan-pole; one bangs a beam, another a wine cask on my head. My legs are covered in mud; soon huge feet trample on me from every side, and a soldier plants his hobnails firmly on my toe. . . .

Up comes a huge trunk of a fir tree swaying on a wagon, and then a dray carrying a whole pine tree; they tower aloft and threaten the people. If the axle of that cart loaded with Ligurian marble breaks and pours its overturned mountain onto the crowd, what is left of their bodies? Who can identify the limbs, who the bones?

Now consider the different and diverse dangers of the night. Just look at the distance down from the rooftop from which a pot comes crack onto my head every time some broken, leaky vessel is pitched out of a window . . . There's death threatening you from every

open window that you pass at night. You are considered stupid and improvident if you go out to dinner without making your will. All you can do is pray that they are content to pour down only the contents of their washing-up basins.

The drunken bully who happens not to have attacked anyone passes a night of torture like that of Achilles mourning his friend, lying now on his face, now on his back; the only way for some men to get any sleep is to pick a fight. Yet, however reckless the fellow may be, however sluiced on wine and hot with young blood, he keeps away from the rich man with scarlet cloak, long retinue of attendants, torches and bronze lamps. But as for me, generally escorted home by the moonlight or the scant light of a candle . . . he pays no respect.

This is how the fight begins – if it is a fight when he does the hitting and I am simply hit. He stands in my way and tells me to stop: I've no option but to obey. What else could I do when I'm faced by a madman? . . . If you try to say anything, if you try to move away silently, it's all the same: he will do you over, and then, in anger, take out a charge against you for assault. Such is the freedom of a poor man: beaten to a jelly, he begs to be allowed to return home with just a few teeth left. ❜

rented rooms in high-rise apartment blocks, known as insulae, or islands, five or six storeys high. The ruins of only a few insulae survive in Rome today, but it is easy in Ostia, the port of Rome, to picture what life was like in the 2nd century AD. In some insulae, a single tenant rented the entire ground floor, living rather as if in a traditional house, or *domus* (for around 30 000 sesterces a year in the 1st century BC). In others, the ground floor was occupied by a series of shops, wine booths and grocery stores, which opened straight onto the street. The family lived and worked in the shop, storing their goods on the ground floor and sleeping on a mezzanine wooden floor built into the back wall, which they reached by a stepladder.

The grander insulae, such as the Insula of Jupiter and Ganymede in Ostia, were rather like mansion blocks today, with splendid apartments of up to ten rooms and perhaps a wooden balcony running round the first floor, from which the residents could watch the sunset or look down on the garden. But living conditions in the one-room apartments on the upper storeys of the poorer insulae were extremely cramped – and not at all cheap (around 2000 sesterces a year in the 1st century

STREET SCENE Roman sellers of fruits, vegetables and herbs set up temporary stalls in the streets on market days, like this stall-holder in Ostia.

BC). There was no running water (the 11 aqueducts that brought more than 200 million gallons of water a day to the city of Rome supplied public rather than private needs), and inhabitants had to use the bath or lavatory on the ground floor – if

LIFE IN THE CITY

there was one – or the public lavatories. They had to fetch water from a nearby well or pay a water-carrier to fetch it for them. The rooms themselves were dark and airless – constantly shaded by the cloths that hung in the windows as some protection from the summer heat or the winter cold. A family might use a charcoal brazier for heating, but this filled the room with smoke and created a considerable fire hazard.

The Romans may have been masterly engineers, but jerrybuilding was rife too. The insulae were especially precarious. There was always the danger – in Rome, in particular – that the poorly built, timber-framed block would simply collapse under the weight of its own storeys. 'Two of my buildings have collapsed,' wrote Cicero, the orator (and slum landlord), 'and in the others the walls are all cracked. Not only the tenants but even the mice have left.' It was for this reason that Emperor Augustus had to limit their height to 70 ft (21 m).

LIFE ON THE STREETS

'There's nowhere a poor man can get any quiet in Rome . . .', complained the Roman poet Martial; and it is clear that the day-to-day noise in the city was appalling. The Romans lived, traded and ate in the street off food cooked on portable stoves and braziers. At night there was the constant rumble of traffic – of draught animals, such as donkeys, mules and oxen, and their drivers. With the exception of heavy goods deliveries of material for the construction of temples and public buildings, traffic had been forbidden during the day since the time of Julius Caesar. Wheeled carriages had to park at the gates of the city – with their passengers walking from there: at the entrance to Ostia, for example, there is a square where the cart drivers parked their vehicles and relaxed in the headquarters, or *collegium,* of their trade association.

Roman cities stank. For example in Pompeii, fish entrails were fermented in open vats under the sun for several months to make *liquamen,* or fish sauce. And passers-by were encouraged to relieve themselves in open jars on the street; the urine was then sold to laundries and to fullers, who used it to dissolve the animal fats and greases in fresh wool.

POOLSIDE MOSAICS An ornamental pool for catching rainwater was a feature of many Roman homes, as in the House with the Mosaic Hall in Herculaneum.

EYEWITNESS

'PARTS OF THE HOUSE WERE OVERLAID WITH GOLD'

AFTER THE GREAT FIRE OF AD 64, the emperor Nero embarked on the building of a vast imperial palace – very little of which is visible today. Here is a description by the historian Suetonius:

❦ His wastefulness showed most of all in the architectural projects. He built a palace, stretching from the Palatine to the Esquiline . . . The following details will give some notion of its size and magnificence. The entrance hall was large enough to contain a huge statue of himself, 120 feet high; and the pillared arcade ran for a whole mile.

EVIL EMPEROR Nero was alleged to have set fire to Rome so that he could rebuild it in great style.

An enormous pool, like a sea, was surrounded by buildings made to resemble cities, and by a landscape garden consisting of ploughed fields, vineyards, pastures, and woodlands – where every variety of domestic and wild animal roamed about. Parts of the house were overlaid with gold and studded with precious stones and mother-of-pearl . . . When the palace had been decorated throughout in this lavish style, Nero dedicated it, and condescended to remark: "Good, now I can at last begin to live like a human being." ❧

MARKET STALL A seller of flowers, fruits and vegetables serves a young customer from his makeshift stall in a typical Roman market.

Although Rome had had a sewage system since the 6th century BC – with drains so massive that you could allegedly drive a loaded wagon through them – they were not equipped with traps: as a result, they often backed up, particularly during floods, and deposited what they were meant to take away. Very few homes had a private lavatory – and those that did were not connected to the drains. Waste simply slopped into a cesspit, where it either seeped into the soil or was dug up and removed every now and then, and sold as manure to market gardeners outside the city. Most people went to public lavatories, where they sat side by side in rows of up to 20 seats.

Going about the unlit streets at night was far from safe. There were only a few nightwatchmen on duty, and so most people stayed in – or, if they had been out to dinner, were accompanied by their slaves. 'Even if you carry only a few plain silver vessels with you on a night journey,' warns the satirist Juvenal, 'you will be terrified of the sword and

RUSH HOUR Scattering pedestrians before it, the horse-drawn carriage in this relief captures the vitality of the streets.

cudgel of the brigand, you will tremble if a reed moves its shadow; but the empty-handed traveller will whistle in the face of the robber.'

THE ROMAN DOMUS

Relatively well-off Romans lived in a one or two-storeyed house known as a *domus*, which turned a blind wall to the sounds and smells of the street. However much they may have liked to recall their rustic origins as shepherds on the Palatine and surrounding hills, the Romans lived very differently by the 3rd century BC. It was hard to recognise in their homes the simple, circular Iron Age huts of their forbears, built of timber supporting a roof of thatch and wattle.

You knocked on the front door with your foot, and entered through a door in the wall which led through the vestibule to an open hall, or atrium,

LIFE AFTER DEATH **The inside of a sarcophagus, found in the Netherlands, was carved to resemble a domestic interior, with furniture and kitchen equipment.**

crouch. Towards the far end of the hall, there was generally a reception room on each side, the *alae*, where masks or busts of the family's ancestors were displayed, and where visitors were entertained. At this end of the hall, you would also find the dining room, or *triclinium* (a room with three wooden or bronze couches arranged in a horseshoe around a table of wood, bronze, stone or silver, with animal's-paw legs); and *tablinum,* where the master of the house conducted business at a portable wooden stool and a tripod table. The wealthier houses and villas, particularly in Rome's colder northern provinces, had a hypocaust, or underfloor central heating system in one of these reception rooms as well as in the bathroom.

On either side of the tablinum and beyond, towards the back of the house, were a jumble of dark, shuttered, or windowless, rooms where the family worked and slept – rooms that were lit rather inefficiently by bronze candelabra or by terracotta lamps, burning olive oil. This is where, in the best preserved Roman cities such as Pompeii, Herculaneum and Ostia, visitors will still find the tiny kitchen with its sink and fireplace, the private lavatory, the storerooms, the baths and the simple

with an ornamental pool in the middle to collect the rainwater. This is where the family worshipped each day at the shrine of the Penates which were thought to protect the home from evil spirits, and where visitors were received. The floors and walls were decorated with mosaic pavements, frescoes and painted statues that drew the visitor's gaze along the central axis of the house to the garden at the rear.

The Romans were different from other Mediterranean peoples in that they preferred to sit down for business and pleasure, rather than squat or

EYEWITNESS

'A BRAZIER GREEN WITH VERDIGRIS'

THE POET MARTIAL describes the possessions of a poor tenant evicted for being in arrears with his rent:
❛ I saw your movables, Vacerra, you disgrace . . . They were not impounded in lieu of two years' rent, so your wife with her seven red curls and your white-haired mother, and your burly sister were carrying them . . . These three went in front and you followed, parched with cold and hunger . . . Along went a three-footed truckle bed and a two-footed table, and a broken chamber pot was pissing from a chip in the side together with a lamp and a cornelwood bowl. The neck of a flagon was lying under a green brazier. An obscenely stinking jug confessed that it had contained salt pickerel or worthless sprats . . . Nor was there wanting a slice of Tolosan cheese, nor a four-year-old wreath of black pennyroyal, nor ropes bare of garlic and onions, nor your mother's pot of foul turpentine . . . This procession of movables is fit for the bridge. ❜

PAINT MAGIC The lavish paint effects – with panels depicting mythological scenes, and columns to create the illusion of architectural perspective – were typical of the wealthier houses in the ancient city of Pompeii.

bedrooms. These would have been sparsely furnished with, perhaps, a chair, a chest, a chamber pot and a wooden bedstead with a straw or reed mattress and some woollen blankets – or for the very rich, a bronze bed with ivory feet, a mattress of wool or down, and a damask quilt.

Right at the back of the house, a portico led into a kitchen garden or – particularly under Greek influence, from the 2nd century BC – into a landscaped pleasure garden surrounded by a peristyle, or colonnade, and planted with evergreen shrubs and flowers, such as roses, poppies and lilies. The gardens featured grottoes, statues, marble fountains fed by aqueducts, and summer dining rooms such as the one at his Tuscan villa in which Pliny the Younger took such pride, floating small dishes of hors d'oeuvres across the surface of the water.

By the 1st century AD, topiary had come into fashion, with box-tree or rosemary hedges sculpted into the shape of wild animals. Such fashions were taken to extremes by the *nouveaux riches* of

OCCASIONAL TABLE This ornate, three-legged, marble-topped table stands on a mosaic pavement in the living room of the House of Paquius Proculus in Pompeii.

Herculaneum and Pompeii who, in an attempt to imitate the country lifestyle of the Roman aristocrats, commissioned vast paintings of wild game animals and populated their gardens with gnome-like bronze fishermen or marble fauns. 'Townsfolk compete with the country houses of Metellus and Lucullus,' the satirist Varro had complained towards the end of the 1st century BC, 'the construction of which was a real public disaster.'

In most Roman cities, the far wall of the peristyle blocked the house off from another street. But, particularly in Herculaneum, which lay on the Mediterranean coast, the wealthier houses had peristyles which opened towards the sea, thus catching the sea breeze and giving the most magnificent views of the Bay of Naples. This open arrangement was a radical architectural departure from the more traditional, inward-looking Roman domus. It was here, on the colonnaded terrace, that their erudite owners could philosophise about the joys of nature.

Many of the features of the traditional Roman domus can be seen, albeit on a more massive and lavish scale, in the palaces of the Roman emperors

DID YOU KNOW?

The Romans were particularly fond of roses. They flavoured their wine with rose petals and powdered their bodies with dried rose petals. The luxury-loving Sybarites (from Sybaris in southern Italy) even made mattresses from rose petals – hence the saying, 'a bed of roses'. At dinners, a rose was sometimes suspended from the ceiling as a sign that everything said beneath it was confidential: hence the Latin phrase *sub rosa*, or 'under the rose'.

'EVERYWHERE THERE IS PEACE AND QUIET'

IN A LETTER to Domitius Apollinaris, who had tried to dissuade him from summering there, the younger Pliny describes the delights of his villa in Tuscany:

❝ . . . So to rid you of all your fears on my account, let me tell you about the climate, the countryside, and the lovely situation of my house, which will be a pleasure alike for me to tell and you to hear . . . From the end of the colonnade projects a dining room; through its folding doors it looks onto the end of the terrace, the adjacent meadow and the stretch of open country beyond . . . Almost opposite the middle of the colonnade is a suite of rooms set slightly back and round a small court shaded by plane trees. In the centre a fountain plays in a marble basin, watering the plane trees round it and the ground beneath them with its light spray . . . At the corner of the colonnade is a large bedroom facing the dining room. Some windows look out onto the terrace, others onto the meadow, while just below the windows in

VILLA HOLIDAY   Seaside villas around the Bay of Naples were popular with the Roman upper classes of the 1st century AD.

front is an ornamental pool. A pleasure both to see and to hear with its water falling from a height and foaming when it strikes the marble. This room is very warm in winter when it is bathed in sunshine and on a cloudy day hot steam from the adjacent furnace room serves instead. Then you pass through a large and cheerful dressing room belonging to the bath, to the cooling room, which contains a good-sized shady swimming bath. If you want

more space to swim or warmer water, there is a pool in the courtyard and a well near to it to tone you up with cold water when you have had enough of the warm . . . I can enjoy a profounder peace there, more comfort and fewer cares. I need never wear a formal toga and there are no neighbours to disturb me. Everywhere there is peace and quiet which adds as much to the healthiness of the place as the clear sky and pure air. ❞

– with rooms arranged around halls and colonnaded garden courtyards. During the Republic, the hill on which Rome's primitive shepherds had first settled became a fashionable residential quarter. The orator Cicero lived there, so did the poet Catullus; and Gaius Octavius, who was to become the first Roman emperor Augustus, was born on the Palatine Hill in 63 BC and later decided to establish his imperial residence there.

Although Augustus's house was relatively modest – in keeping with a man who, according to the historian Suetonius wore homemade clothes, used the same bedroom for 40 years, and preferred the food of the common people – those of his successors were not. They covered almost the entire Palatine (from which the word palace derives). The

emperor Domitian's enormous palace, which was built towards the end of the 1st century AD, was both a public residence and a private home. It had a hall of justice with marble walls, a private stadium and a massive pool with a gallery whose walls, according to Suetonius, 'were lined with plaques of highly polished moonstone, which reflected everything that happened behind his back' (these failed to save the paranoid emperor from being murdered in his bedroom). There were sunken gardens, carpeted with roses, violets, myrtle, rue and acanthus; a vast dining room with a mosaic floor and walls of pink marble; and magnificent views from the imperial box over the horse-racing in the Circus Maximus and towards the silhouette of undulating Alban Hills on the horizon.

WALKING IN THE PAST

Graffiti daubed on the walls of Pompeii allow the modern

visitor to eavesdrop on the ancients.

WANDERING AROUND the ruined streets of ancient Pompeii today, you can almost overhear the conversations of a couple of thousand years ago. For the public events and private passions of the people are recorded in the graffiti painted or scratched on the walls and stones. They range from the potentially libellous – 'Lucius Statius Philadelphus, freedman of Gaia, is a thief' – to the positively lyrical – 'Nothing lasts for ever. After shining brightly, the sun sinks into the ocean; the moon which was full, waxes. The fury of the wind often changes into the gentle breeze.'

There are announcements of

VOTE CATCHER   An inscription on a street wall in Pompeii promotes the candidature of a man called Lollius, who stood for election as aedile in AD 78.

births, deaths and of public honours; offers of reward for the return of stolen goods; official notices forbidding illegal building; for rent signs; and advertisements for gladiatorial games – 'On the 25th and 26th of February, in Pompeii, there will be a show by Tiberius Claudius Verus, including combat against wild beasts, wrestling matches and sprinkling with scented water, offered for the health of Nero Claudius Caesar Augustus Germanicus.' Most of the painted

PEDESTRIAN CROSSING   Stepping stones cross a street in Pompeii, allowing pedestrians to rise above the mud and rubbish that clogged the street.

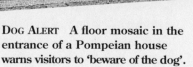

DOG ALERT   A floor mosaic in the entrance of a Pompeian house warns visitors to 'beware of the dog'.

LOVE LETTERS Several graffiti, written by different people, clamour for attention on a wall; most are messages of love.

inscriptions are, however, election posters for candidates for the city magistracies – along the lines of 'In Nuceria, vote for Lucius Munatius Caesernius . . . he is an honest man'. At night professional sign-writers would arrive with a ladder and brush, and lime-wash the wall before drawing red or black characters on it.

Just as in Italian cities today, there are notices of markets: 'Markets are held in Pompeii and Nuceria on Saturdays, at Atella and Nola on Sundays, at Cumae on Mondays, in Puteoli on Tuesdays, in Rome on Wednesdays and in Capua on Thursdays . . .' Individual traders advertise their wares and warn their less reliable clients: 'I hate the poor. Anybody who asks for something free is crazy; pay the price and get the goods.'

Sometimes the complaints come from the customers, like this one: 'Would that you pay for all your tricks, innkeeper. You sell us water

and keep the good wine for yourself.' But it is the more personal messages that are the most poignant. Scratched on the tomb of an ancient warrior, along with the more formal references to distant campaigns, are the words: 'Atimetus got me pregnant.' There is Novella Primigenia, the girl from Nuceria, to whom one suitor wrote: 'For just one hour I'd like to be the stone of this ring, to give to you who moisten it with your mouth, the kisses I have impressed on it.' In another part of Pompeii, on the walls of the Basilica, a disappointed lover threatens revenge on Venus, the goddess of love: 'Whoever loves, go to hell. I want to break Venus's ribs with blows and deform her hips. If she can break my tender heart,

ELECTION SLOGAN Painted on a building in Pompeii, this election message would have been the work of a specialist sign writer.

why can't I hit her over the head?'

Sometimes the messages were written inside the house, rather than on the street, such as the host who requested on his dining-room walls that guests should: 'Avoid making lustful faces and languid eyes at the wives of others' . . . and 'Avoid arguments and postpone unpleasant quarrels, if you can; otherwise, leave and go home.'

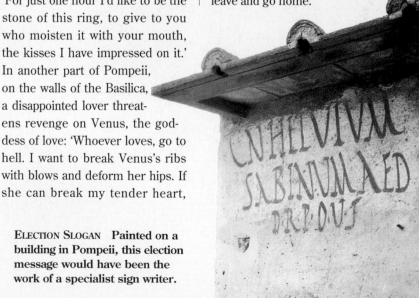

LIFE ON THE STREET

THE STATUE of a Roman general overlooks the bustle of a busy crossroads. At his feet, children play a form of dice, using animal knucklebones, while their parents draw water from a public fountain. Animals root in the rubbish that clogs the streets, forcing pedestrians to pick their way along stepping stones. Only the wealthy, carried in their canopied litters by slaves, could rise above it completely.

The Romans lived most of their lives on the street, trading and selling food and drink from open-fronted shops on the ground floor of multistoreyed apartment blocks (right). On the first floor, citizens survey the scene from a balcony while others, less helpfully, toss their refuse onto the street below. Other everyday hazards included fires that ravaged whole areas of the city.

CLOTHES AND COSMETICS

Following fashions set by their leaders, the Romans abandoned

the severe and simple styles of the Republic for the

eye-catching extravagance and sartorial status symbols of the Empire.

WITH THE POSSIBLE exception of their public nakedness at the baths, the Romans were a modest people. Most of them went to bed in their underclothes: for men, a linen loincloth and a short-sleeved, knee-length tunic, consisting of two pieces of cloth, stitched together with holes for the head and arms and tied at the waist with a belt; and for Roman women, a breast-band as well.

When they got up in the morning, all they had to do was to drape a cloak or another tunic on top and to put on their leather sandals. Depending on the weather, they might wear more than one tunic – the emperor Augustus, a martyr to cold, is believed to have worn four tunics at a time.

THE CITIZEN'S UNIFORM

In the city – and certainly if he was going to a public function – the Roman citizen had to wear the traditional cloak, the toga, over the tunic. Its colour denoted the citizen's social status.

For example, the ordinary adult wore a plain, brownish toga, the natural colour of the wool from which it was made. An election candidate might

HOW TO TIE A TOGA

THE ROMAN TOGA consisted of a huge semicircle of unbleached wool, up to 18 ft (5.5 m) in diameter. To put it on, you supported one end of the straight edge on your left arm so that about a third of the material hung in front. You then drew the straight edge round across the left shoulder and back, and under the right arm. Finally, you threw it back over the left shoulder where it hung in flowing folds – thereby leaving the right arm free but restricting movement of the left arm.

TOGA PARTY **A stately procession of priests and senators illustrates how the toga should be worn.**

wear a bright white, bleached toga; an augur or religious official, a saffron-coloured one; a senior magistrate or senator, the *toga praetexta*, edged with a thick band of purple (the dye came from seashells such as murex); a censor an all-purple toga; and a victorious general, a purple toga edged with gold.

The toga, however, was fiddly to arrange (you needed a wife or a slave to help to put it on); and, although the way it restricted rapid movement lent a certain gravitas to the wearer, it was extremely uncomfortable and cumbersome. It was difficult to run or fight when wearing one.

The poet Martial lists having to wear a toga only occasionally as one of the constituents of a happy life, along with good health and inherited wealth. It is hardly surprising then that, by imperial times, the toga was going out of fashion; emperors such as Claudius vainly issued decrees ordering them to be worn by men of rank at certain times. It was replaced by a simpler cloak, the *amictus,* for off-duty occasions. Increasingly, when citizens went out in the late afternoon to dine, they tended to wear the *synthesis,* a cross between the toga and the tunic.

In 195 BC a demonstration of women through the streets of Rome had led to the repeal of the Oppian Law which had forbidden women to wear dyed clothes or to own more than an ounce of gold.

This loosening of the ban on extravagance unleashed hundreds of years of acute fashion-consciousness among rich Roman women – to the disapproval of the moralists.

Having donned her slippers and her long dress or *stola*, and enamelled her teeth with powdered horn, dressing her hair was the wealthy Roman

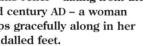

STONE MAIDEN
In this relief – dating from the 2nd century AD – a woman steps gracefully along in her sandalled feet.

49

wife's first priority. This was the task of her personal maid, the *ornatrix*, using a comb of bronze, bone, ivory, tortoiseshell or even gold. The headdress was styled with a rod-shaped curling iron heated over burning coals; hairpins and nets and unguents were added. And the effect could be admired in a mirror of glass laid over a reflective metal. The ornatrix also applied the elaborate daily make-up, which was sold in ceramic vases, glass phials or alabaster pots. First, she applied foundation, made from lanolin (the grease from unwashed sheep's wool), before painting antimony powder (as mascara) around the eyes, red paint on the lips and cheeks, and white lead or chalk on the face.

The painted lady then chose her jewels – perhaps a diadem, earrings, bracelets, anklets and rings – and finally completed dressing, putting on her long upper tunic and her *pallium*, a dazzlingly coloured cloak, made from either cotton or Chinese silk and dyed white with chalk, blue with woad or yellow with saffron. She carried a cloth called a *mappa* dangling from her wrist, which she used to dab dust or perspiration from her face.

A young man's first shave was marked by a religious ceremony – the *depositio barbae* – which normally coincided with the first wearing of the adult toga, the *toga virilis*. Roman men rarely combed their own hair or shaved themselves. The rich would have a slave perform the task at home every day. But most people would allow a few days' growth of beard – never, between the 1st century BC and the days of Emperor Hadrian (AD 117-38), a long beard – and then visit one of the many barbers' shops scattered throughout the city. From dawn to what the Romans defined as the eighth hour (12.44 to 1.29 in winter, 1.15 to 2.31 in summer), these were constantly crowded. Clients sat waiting on benches, looking at themselves in the mirrors arranged around the walls, and gossiped.

Roman men generally favoured a short, no-nonsense haircut. For ordinary haircuts, the barbers, or *tonsores*, used a pair of primitive iron scissors, without a pivot in the middle – with the result that many haircuts were fairly rough-and-ready. Elegant young men, on the other hand, had their hair curled artificially with curling irons, which had previously been heated in their metal sheaths. And the truly vain or fashion-conscious had hair dye, made from natural substances such as henna, applied, along with perfume and make-up cream for the cheeks. Sometimes little patches of cloth were

BEAUTY AIDS
A fresco from the 1st century AD shows a woman pouring perfume into a phial (left). The wood and ivory toiletry set (below) held chalk and white lead to lighten the complexion, ash or antimony for eye make-up and red ochre for the lips.

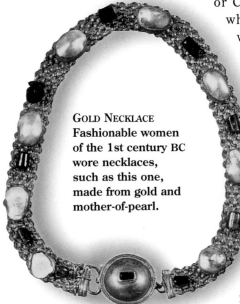

GOLD NECKLACE
Fashionable women of the 1st century BC wore necklaces, such as this one, made from gold and mother-of-pearl.

PAINTED LADY The jewellery worn by this beautiful young woman from Egypt is typical of 2nd-century fashions.

CURLS, BEARDS AND FRINGES FOR THE FASHION-CONSCIOUS

FASHION PARADE The elaborate hairstyles featured in the middle of this line up were typical of the 1st century AD.

ROMAN STATUES can be dated quite precisely by the type of hairstyle worn by the women.

During the Republic, for example, they favoured a simple style, parted in the middle with possibly a fringe of curls resting on the forehead and fastened at the back in a bun. Next came a fashion, adopted by women of the imperial family such as Livia and Octavia in the early 1st century AD, for hair that ran either side of a central parting to form ringlets over the ears, with a lock of hair brushed forward in a wave over the forehead and a chignon at the nape of the neck. Later that century, there was a vogue for hair piled elaborately high in spiral curls – as popular with the women around the time of the Flavian emperors (AD 69-96).

'So numerous are the tiers and storeys piled one upon another on

BOWL CUT Closely cropped hair was favoured by this man.

her head!' wrote Juvenal in his satire on women: 'In front, you would take her for an Andromache; she is not so tall behind; you would not think it was the same person.' Indeed, so fashion-conscious were the Romans that some sculpted portrait busts had removable stone wigs, to anticipate any future changes in style.

Much the same was true for men, as hairstyles and the wearing of beards followed the fashions set by the emperors. The manly, slightly scruffy hairstyle favoured by the emperor Augustus gradually gave way to Nero's taste for waved hair and sideburns, Trajan's carefully tonsured bob, and Hadrian's neat beard and curled locks.

carefully stuck to the skin to hide blemishes or to enhance a poor complexion.

The beard was trimmed with a pair of scissors, and then the agony of shaving with a clumsy iron razor began. There was no shaving cream or soap to soften the skin – only water. Cuts and gashes were so frequent that Pliny the Elder recorded for posterity the plaster that was used to staunch bleeding: it consisted of spiders' webs soaked in oil and vinegar. The most fastidious Romans even resorted to plucking the bristles from the chin with tweezers.

Cowardly – or prudent – Romans took to depilatories, such as a liniment made of resin and pitch; alternatively, the face could be rubbed with *psilothrum*, an ingredient procured from the white vine, or some other paste, concocted from ivy gum, bat's blood, or powdered viper.

HEALTH AND HYGIENE

For the Romans, bathing was firstly a sacred and then a social ritual. From ancient times they had washed before entering a sanctuary or embarking

COMMUNAL CONVENIENCE In town, the ancient Romans used public lavatories – a row of holes sited over a drain.

on any religious activity. However, by the time of the empire, the afternoon visit to the public baths – and the removal of the dirt from the pores of the skin with a scraper known as a strigil – was an integral part of the citizen's social round. Moralists recalled in vain that era when the bath had served a purpose: when, according to the philosopher Seneca, Scipio 'did not bathe in filtered water; it was often turbid, and after heavy rains almost muddy! But it did not matter much to Scipio if he had to bathe in that way; he went there to wash off sweat, not ointment'. By the 1st century AD, the bath was part of a more elaborate ritual upon which, according to the satirist Juvenal, 'your great man will spend six hundred sesterces'.

For whichever reason – religion or relaxation – the Romans were generally quite clean. Indeed, they often associated cleanliness with health (and godliness): the two deities most often represented in the public baths were Aesculapius, the Roman god of medicine, and Hygieia, the goddess of health. In this they were rather mistaken. There is no

evidence that disinfectant was used in the public baths, and the water itself was probably changed only quite rarely. Furthermore, the writer Celsus, whose eight books on *Medicine* formed part of a large encyclopaedia, showed no understanding of the dangers of contagion by recommending that people visit the baths to treat liver abscesses, cholera, dysentery, worm infestations, bowel ailments, rabies and boils, among other complaints. The oils, greases and perfumes with which people anointed themselves after the baths did nothing to counteract these.

The public lavatories, too, must have been a breeding ground for bacteria. There were few facilities for washing and, instead of toilet paper, people generally used a sponge on a stick which was then washed after use and re-used. Other aspects of an individual's toilet included cleaning the ears with vinegar and the teeth with a bicarbonate of soda mixture, although the poet Catullus also mentions with disgust the habit of Egnatius the Spaniard who scrubbed his teeth with urine to make them glisten.

INSIDE THE HOME

CLIENTS SIT on a bench outside a wealthy citizen's home, waiting to be admitted to an early morning audience with their patron. Having passed through the vestibule, they might have proceeded to an open hall, the atrium, where an ornamental pool to catch the rainwater is set into a floor of richly decorated mosaics. Reception rooms lead off the atrium, but the most privileged guests would have continued along the central garden to the peristyle, a colonnaded courtyard filled with flowers. Back on the street, servants gather around the side entrance to the house; this leads to the servants' quarters, including the kitchen, from which smoke rises through an upstairs window.

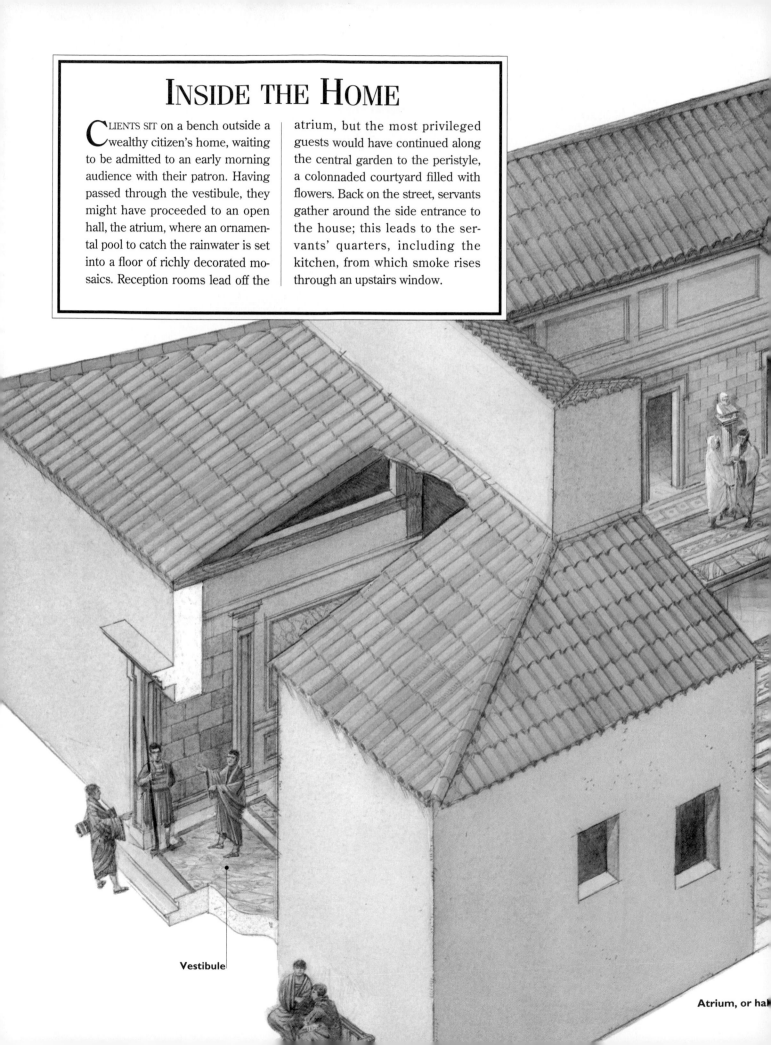

Vestibule

Atrium, or ha

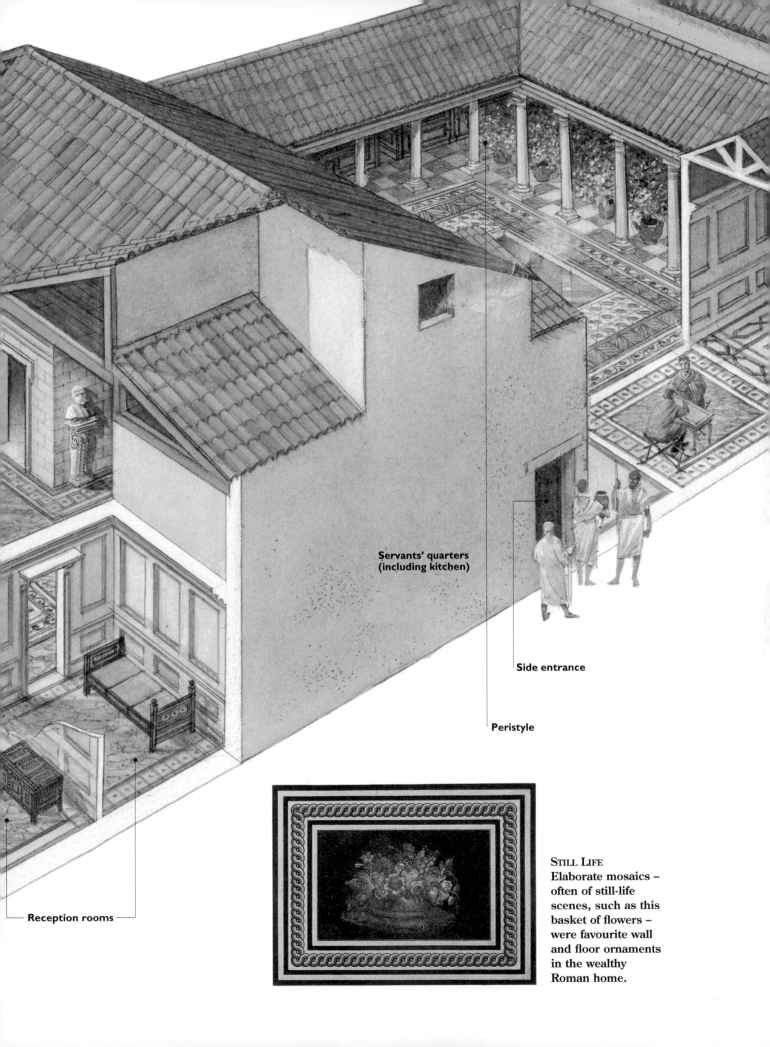

Servants' quarters
(including kitchen)

Side entrance

Peristyle

Reception rooms

STILL LIFE
Elaborate mosaics –
often of still-life
scenes, such as this
basket of flowers –
were favourite wall
and floor ornaments
in the wealthy
Roman home.

FOOD AND DRINK

For a people whose roots were so firmly planted in the soil of central Italy,

the Romans developed a surprising taste for heavily spiced and exotic foods,

presented with a great sense of theatre.

ACCORDING TO SUETONIUS, the palace official and biographer of 'the twelve Caesars', Emperor Vitellius (AD 69), who banqueted up to four times a day, enjoyed a particular dish of pike livers, pheasant brains, peacock brains and flamingo-tongues: ingredients that had to be 'brought to Rome by naval captains and triremes'.

But despite such tales of gargantuan appetites and elaborate banquets, the Romans were in general a frugal people who prided themselves on their rustic origins and simple tastes. This was certainly the attitude of Juvenal, the great Roman satirist, who bemoaned the fact that the Romans of his day had forgotten many of the simple pleasures and foods of their forefathers. And doctors and moralists, too, constantly counselled moderation and condemned those who were slaves to their passions.

THE DAILY DIET

Breakfast consisted of little more than bread and fruit. The midday meal might be some leftovers of cold meat and vegetables such as lentils, lettuce, leeks, carrots or celery, some eggs, or simply a snack snatched standing up at a bar. Olives were particularly popular – just as in a Roman market today, they came in a range of types, sizes and pickles – and could be purchased in a cornet made of papyrus from a street vendor. Other favourite snacks included roasted meat cubes, sprats, sausages, fried fish, pies and proteins such as beans, lentils and lupin seeds.

Very few Romans went without their daily bread. From 71 BC, free grain was distributed to Rome's poor, and at the height of the Roman Empire, 100 or more years later, at least a third of the inhabitants of the imperial city were on the dole. Successive emperors increased the *annona*, as it was known, to include ready-made bread rather than grain, along with pork fat and even wine.

To fulfil the demand, the Romans shipped wheat to Rome from fields in Sicily, North Africa (a four-day journey) and Egypt (13 days). The grain was then milled on a massive scale in rotary

DONKEY WORK
Attached to a shaft, a donkey rotates a quernstone, used in the milling of flour.

DELIGHTS OF THE TABLE   Coloured glassware would have graced many a wealthy Roman table in the 1st century AD.

querns: the commercial mill consisted of a conical base stone and a hollow, hour-glass shaped upper stone attached to a shaft pulled by a donkey. The animal plodded round and round in circles, rotating the upper stone against the base stone, thereby milling the grain. This was baked into a whole range of breads: from the plainest varieties, which you might dip in wine for a midday snack, to honey-and-oil breads or loaves flavoured with aniseed and cheese.

The evening meal, or *cena*, was the only real social occasion. People generally ate this after a visit to the baths at the end of the ninth hour (4 pm) in summer, and an hour earlier in winter. Both the recipes and the rituals depended on whether you were a peasant in the countryside or an aristocrat in Rome. It might be as basic as bean purée and a porridge made from millet or chickpea flour (rather like the polenta of today), with some

HARVEST TIME   Labourers gather the apple harvest on a typical estate in ancient Gaul in the 2nd or 3rd century AD.

bacon or a chicken from the farmyard on special occasions. Or it might take the form of a full three-course meal served in an elegant Roman domus.

The first course generally included eggs and olives. Then came the main course, which consisted of up to seven different dishes, such as chicken, wild boar, hare, or sows' udders. Italy, in those days, was heavily wooded: which explains the availability – and popularity – of wild game such as venison, pheasant and partridge. These dishes would be announced and explained, as in some contemporary restaurants, by an attendant. Dessert, consisting of honey cakes or fruit, completed this progression 'from the eggs to the apples', as the poet Horace described it.

With any luck, the guests would receive the same food as their host – unlike the unfortunate diners described by Juvenal who were served with 'a prawn, hemmed in by half an egg, crouched on a tiny saucer, a meal fit for a ghost', while their host ate a massive lobster 'walled around with choice asparagus'. Discrimination such as this was quite common in ancient Rome, where wealthy patrons would demean their clients by placing them on a stool, instead of a couch, or in a lowly position around the table.

THE ROMAN BANQUET

Deducing what the Romans ate regularly from 1st-century accounts of Roman feasts would be as misleading as basing a description of the 20th-century diet on the cookery books of a fashionable chef of to-day. Nevertheless, the food at banquets was much more elaborate than the everyday meals – and the rituals, too, were designed to lend a sense of dignity to the occasion. They were a great opportunity for people to show off.

On their way to the feast, guests might pop into a shop selling perfume or wreaths of olive or bay leaves for their heads; alternatively, the host might supply these on arrival, along with thin sandals which were removed just before the meal. Guests would change into a *synthesis*, a combination of

tunic and shawl (it was considered smart to bring several of these along to dinner). And then there would be a small ceremony in which the diners poured some wine as an offering to the household gods – or even, at times of national emergency, presented them with a whole meal.

Many of Rome's dining rooms were utterly magnificent. According to Suetonius, the emperor Nero had 'ceilings of fretted ivory, the panels of which could slide back and let a rain of flowers, or of perfume from hidden sprinklers, shower upon his guests. The main dining room was circular, and its roof revolved, day and night, in time with the sky.' Guests lounged three to a couch, propping themselves up on their left elbows and therefore – like many cultures today – eating exclusively with their right hand. The three couches were arranged in a horseshoe shape around a central table, one side of which was left free for the service of food. As with so many aspects of Roman life, the allotment of

FAST FOOD Snacks, such as sausages, and drinks, generally wine, were served at the counter of this shop in Pompeii; the jars were for storing oil and wine.

'LET'S EAT, IF YOU DON'T MIND'

IN *The Satyricon*, the 1st-century author and imperial official, Petronius, caricatures a feast of gluttony hosted by the fictional self-made millionaire Trimalchio in a seaside town in Campania.

❡ Finally we took our places. Boys from Alexandria poured iced water over our hands. Others followed them and attended to our feet, removing any hangnails with great skill . . . Some extremely elegant hors d'oeuvres were served at this point . . . an ass of Corinthian bronze with two panniers, white olives on one side and black on the other. Over the ass were two pieces of plate, with Trimalchio's name and the weight of the silver inscribed on the rims. There were some small iron frames shaped like bridges supporting dormice sprinkled with honey and poppy seed. There were steaming hot sausages too, on a silver gridiron with damsons and pomegranate seeds underneath . . . While we were still on the hors d'oeuvres, a tray was brought in with a basket on it. There sat a wooden hen, its wings spread round it the way hens are when they are broody. Two slaves hurried up and as the orchestra played a tune they began searching through the straw and dug out peahens' eggs, which they distributed to the guests . . . We took up our spoons (weighing at least half a pound each) and cracked the eggs, which were made of rich pastry . . . I searched the shell with my fingers and found the plumpest little figpecker [a small bird], all covered

BIRD FOOD A clutch of thrushes are hung to provide a delicacy.

with yolk and seasoned with pepper . . . Carefully sealed wine bottles were immediately brought, their necks labelled "FALERNIAN CONSUL OPIMIUS ONE HUNDRED YEARS OLD" [a supposedly vintage wine] . . . Naturally we drank and missed no opportunity of admiring his elegant hospitality . . . After our applause the next course was brought in. Actually it was not as grand as we expected, but it was so novel that everyone stared. It was a deep circular tray with the twelve signs of the Zodiac arranged around the edge. Over each of them the chef had placed some appropriate dainty suggested by the subject. Over Aries the Ram, chickpeas; over Taurus the Bull, a beefsteak; over the Heavenly Twins, testicles and kidneys; over Cancer the Crab, a garland; over Leo the Lion, an African fig; over Virgo the Virgin, a young sow's udder; over Libra the Scales, a balance with a cheesecake in one pan and a pastry in the other; over Scorpio, a sea scorpion; over Capricorn, a lobster;

over Aquarius the Water-carrier, a goose; over Pisces the Fishes, two mullets. In the centre was a piece of grassy turf bearing a honeycomb . . . As we started rather reluctantly on this inferior fare, Trimalchio said: "Let's eat, if you don't mind. This is the sauce of all order." As he spoke, four dancers hurtled forward in time to the music and removed the upper part of the great dish, revealing underneath plump fowls, sows' udders, and a hare with wings fixed to the middle to look like Pegasus [a winged horse]. We also noticed four figures of Marsyas [a satyr] with little skin bottles, which let a peppery fish-sauce go running over some fish, which seemed to be swimming in a little channel . . . Then the servants came up and laid across the couches embroidered coverlets showing nets, hunters carrying broad spears, and all the paraphernalia of hunting. We were still wondering which way to look when a tremendous clamour arose outside the dining room, and surprise! – Spartan hounds began dashing everywhere, even round the table. behind them came a great dish and on it lay a wild boar of the largest possible size, and, what is more, wearing a freedman's cap on its head. From its tusks dangled two baskets woven from palm leaves, one full of fresh Syrian dates, the other of dried Theban dates . . . A huge bearded fellow . . . pulled out a hunting knife and made a great stab at the boar's side and, as he struck, out flew a flock of thrushes. ❡

guests to couches was governed by an elaborate protocol: the couch of honour was the one opposite the empty side of the table; the one to the right of this was the next most honourable, followed by the one to the left.

Although they used spoons for eating soft foods and sauces and pronged spoons for extracting seafood from shells, the Romans generally ate with their hands or used platforms of bread to transfer food to their mouths. This is why Roman food was never served too hot and why it was usually solid. They would wipe their fingers on one of two napkins, which they had brought with them to the dinner – the other would be tied around their neck. At the end of the meal, the host gave food to each of his guests to take away, wrapped in the napkin he had brought with him.

On rare occasions, the banquet might last up to ten hours, from four o'clock in the afternoon into the early hours of the morning, with the intervals between courses enlivened with gambling and dancing girls, music and acrobatic turns. This was exactly the type of entertainment that the priggish official Pliny, who preferred more intellectual pastimes, disparaged in a letter to a friend: '. . . I have nothing of that kind in my own house, but I can put up with those who do. The reason why I don't have them is that I find nothing novel or amusing to attract me in that sort of dancer's charms, in a mime's impudence, or a clown's folly.'

Apart from a few sips of wine or water to wash down the food, real drinking began

MAKING READY Romans prepare for a banquet in this detail from a mosaic floor found in the North African city of Carthage.

WAITER SERVICE A servant carries a plate bearing a boar's head into a Roman banquet.

only after the dishes had been cleared. Pitchers of wine and water, and coolers packed with snow, would be brought in and guests would settle down to the ceremonial drinking bout, known as the *commissatio* – and to hours of discussion of issues both lofty and low.

Some of the table manners may seem strange to us. Belching was considered a gesture of appreciation – as it is with the Arabs today – and it was said that Emperor Claudius (AD 41-54) even wanted to pass an edict permitting people to break wind freely at table. There are even stories of greedy diners making room for the next assault of courses by tickling the back of their throat with a peacock feather. So disgusted by this habit was the philosopher Seneca that he observed that 'they vomit to eat and eat to vomit'.

A TASTE OF ROME

Historians have been able to reconstruct something about Roman cooking methods from ancient recipe books. Meat and fish were generally boiled in a cauldron suspended over an open fire, or roasted on spits over a charcoal barbecue or in an oven made of rubble and tiles. It was then served on plates of silver or pewter (or, for the less well-off, of pottery, glass or bronze) and drowned in spicy sauces. Two of the ten books which constitute the gourmet Apicius's work are devoted to fish and sauces to accompany fish, such as date and thyme sauce for poached tuna. There was a very good reason for this.

In the 1st century AD, Rome had a population of more than a million – making it, until the 20th century, the largest Mediterranean city in history. Spread over an area about a quarter the size of present-day Paris, the city lost direct contact with the surrounding countryside unlike other, smaller ancient centres of population. Although vegetables were cultivated in the suburbs and were therefore fresh, meat and fish generally came from farther afield. Transport was slow, and food had to be stored, unrefrigerated, in warehouses where it went off quite quickly. Wealthy Romans coped with this problem, up to a point, by keeping fish alive in private fishponds or by rearing birds such as thrushes in aviaries and domestic fowl such as chickens and capons in battery cages. But the simplest way to hide the rancid taste of old meat was to spice it heavily – with the result that much Roman food was hot or sweet-and-sour in flavour (for example, slices of veal served in a sauce of raisins, honey, pepper, onions, cheap wine and herbs).

Roman food was heavily seasoned with salt; with herbs, such as parsley, lovage, rue, rosemary and dill; and with spices not indigenous to the Mediterranean, such as Indian pepper (which was even used to flavour homemade biscuits or honey omelette). Cinnamon, ginger, cumin, cardamom, nutmeg and cloves came from as far away as India, China and Indonesia. At one point, spices represented 44 out of 88 types of goods imported to Rome from Africa and Asia – along with parrots and eunuchs – in exchange for the products of the Roman Empire such as glassware, linen, coral, gems and, above all, gold and silver. There was also the pungent juice of the giant fennel, known as *asafoetida*, which was imported from North Africa and the Middle East. 'The number of uses is immeasurable', wrote Pliny; for not only was it used as a seasoning but also as a diuretic, a healing ointment for sores, snakebites and scorpion stings, and as a cure for corns, carbuncles and cramp.

But most distinctive of all the seasonings was a clear fermented fish sauce called *liquamen* which was made from rotting fish guts and tasted not unlike sauces such as *nam pla* that are found in Far Eastern cooking today. Here is a recipe for liquamen: 'Place fish guts in a bowl and salt them: add anchovies, small mullets, picarels, sprats and every other sort of tiny fish, and salt them as well; set the fish in the sun so that the salt melts and the fish are marinated in the solution; and turn them often. When they are thoroughly sopped . . . put them through a sieve . . .' The most desirable brands, it was thought, were produced in Leptis Magna (in Libya), Antipolis (present-day Antibes) and Pompeii.

DESIGNER FOOD

Just as Roman cooks did all they could to disguise the taste of the food, they also often transformed how it looked – with a great sense of theatre. Hams were made to resemble turtledoves; knuckles of pork to look like chicken; and pig was stuffed with other creatures and known as Trojan pig, after the

---

EYEWITNESS

'... AND WINE WITH HONEY CHILLED WITH SNOW'

PLINY THE YOUNGER, the lawyer and landowner, rebukes a friend for failing to turn up for dinner:

❛ Who are you to accept my invitation to dinner and never come? . . . It was all laid out, one lettuce each, three snails, two eggs, barley-cake, and wine with honey chilled with snow . . . besides olives, beetroots, gherkins, onions, and any number of similar delicacies. You would have heard a comic play, a reader or singer, or all three if I felt generous. Instead you chose to go where you could have oysters, sow's innards, sea urchins, and Spanish dancing girls. You will suffer for this – I won't say how. ❜

RECIPES FROM ANCIENT ROME

Most of what we know about Roman cookery comes from the writings of a wealthy 1st-century gastronome called Caelius Apicius. Here are a few recipes adapted from *De Re Coquinaria* (On Cookery) and later Roman cookbooks: one, a *gustatio* or taster; three *fercula* or main courses; and a *secunda mensa* (literally, 'second table') or dessert. Quantities are for four people.

IN MITULIS (OF MUSSELS)

0.9 kg (2 lb) mussels
3 tablespoons chopped chives
1/2 teaspoon cumin
250 ml (9 fl oz) white wine
250 ml (9 fl oz) water

1. Put the mussels in cold water for 30 minutes and discard any that remain open. Clean the mussels, removing the beards.
2. Place the mussels in a saucepan with the chopped chives, cumin, wine and water.
3. Bring to the boil and then simmer for 5 minutes.

PULLUM LASERATUM

(CHICKEN WITH GINGER)
1.8 kg (4 lb) chicken
1/2 teaspoon black peppercorns
1/2 teaspoon celery seeds
1 teaspoon ground ginger
250 ml (9 fl oz) chicken stock
125 ml (4 fl oz) white wine

STORAGE SPACE A wall painting from Pompeii proclaims the Roman taste for the good things of life: a bowl of eggs, a wine jug, and a clutch of thrushes.

1. Place the chicken in a casserole.
2. Grind together the peppercorns, celery seeds and ginger; mix this with the stock and white wine and pour over the chicken.
3. Bring to the boil on top of the oven, and simmer gently for 1¼ hours until the chicken is poached.

ALITER LENTICULUM

(LENTILS AND LEEKS)
250 ml (9 fl oz) lentils
2 leeks, sliced
1/2 teaspoon coriander seeds
sprig of rosemary
1 teaspoon chopped, fresh mint
1 teaspoon wine vinegar
1 tablespoon honey
125 ml (4 fl oz) vegetable stock
125 ml (4 fl oz) white wine

1. Cover the lentils in water and cook for about 30 minutes. Add the leeks and cook until tender. Drain.
2. Meanwhile, grind together the coriander, rosemary and mint; and mix with the vinegar, honey, vegetable stock and wine. Combine with the lentils and leeks, and bring slowly to the boil. Serve.

HOG ROAST A mosaic from the Roman city of Trier in Germany shows a servant bearing a roast pig to the table.

PISAM SIVE FABAM VITELLIANAM

(PEAS OR BEANS VITELLIAN)
700 g (1 lb 9 oz) peas or beans
pinch pepper
pinch ginger
2 hard-boiled egg yolks
3 tablespoons honey
1 teaspoon anchovy essence
1 tablespoon wine
1 tablespoon vinegar
1 tablespoon olive oil

1. Boil the peas until soft; then drain and purée until smooth.
2. Pound together the pepper, ginger and hard-boiled egg yolks and, in a saucepan, mix with the honey, anchovy essence, wine, vinegar and olive oil. Bring to the boil.
3. Add the pea purée and simmer for several minutes, stirring gently.

OVA SPONGIA EX LACTE

(EGG SPONGE IN MILK)
6 eggs
350 ml (12 fl oz) milk
15 g (1/2 oz) butter
3 tablespoons liquid honey
1/2 teaspoon ground cinnamon

1. Beat the eggs and milk together.
2. Melt the butter in a frying pan over a medium heat; pour in the mixture of egg and milk, and cook gently for several minutes.
3. When the omelette is almost set, spoon in the honey and sprinkle with cinnamon. Serve immediately.

ancient Greek story of the wooden Trojan horse which concealed the soldiers who captured the city of Troy. There is an account of a meal that Emperor Heliogabalus served his guests, which featured 600 ostrich brains, peas mixed with grains of gold, and lentils with precious stones.

To the great ridicule of Roman satirists, wealthy hosts slavishly followed fashions or sought to outdo each other by creating new recipes or championing new delicacies, such as sturgeon, stork, mullet (for 6000 sesterces, according to one of Juvenal's satires), milk-fed snails, nightingales, turbot, oysters from Britain, and dormice fattened in pottery vessels on acorns and chestnuts.

WINE ON TAP In a tavern scene from a 1st-century funerary relief, a man draws wine from a barrel.

IN VINO VERITAS

The ancient Romans generally drank their wine diluted with an equal measure of water (occasionally sea water or ice transported by donkey-pack from the Alps and then stored in underground caves). Even so, they sometimes drank it in prodigious quantities: the poet Martial, for example, described how he quaffed 5 pints (2.8 litres) in a single evening.

Although vines had been grown in southern Italy as early as 800 BC and in northern Italy by the Etruscans, the Romans first got seriously interested in wine around 200 BC – both for personal pleasure and for profit.

The coast between Naples and Sorrento became fashionable for wealthy Romans, who built themselves sumptuous villas overlooking the sea. They began to take over the old Greek vineyards, producing their own top-quality wines for the first time and, rather like the wine chateaux of Bordeaux today, creating a wine industry that was centred around individual villas. The most famous of these 'first-growths' was Falernian.

All these wines were amber in colour and would have tasted strong and sweet – much like Madeira or Marsala today. But such was the Roman taste for seasoning that they flavoured them further with honey (the Romans did not have sugar), rose petals, mint and pepper.

The taste for wine was not restricted to people like the fictional millionaire Trimalchio, who appreciated great vintages such as the 'Opimian' vintage of 121 BC (the year when Opimius was consul).

A stroll around the ruined streets of Pompeii reveals some 200 buildings that are recognisable as bars – in one of which you can even read the price of the wine from a list on the wall.

Poor people, on the other hand, had to content themselves with a mixture of vinegar (from wine that had gone sour) and water – which was what the Roman soldiers offered Jesus Christ on the Cross.

Wine became increasingly popular throughout Italy. By the turn of the millennium, Rome was importing vast quantities from Campania – a trade which came to an abrupt halt when, in AD 79, Mount Vesuvius erupted, burying Pompeii and the surrounding vineyards under several yards of ash. Soon Romans were trying to establish vineyards nearer to home or importing thinner, drier white wines – for which they had developed a taste – from northern Italy and Gaul.

A FINE VINTAGE

To this day, a couple of southern Italy's most distinguished wines are made from vines that were probably imported from Greece before the Roman colonisation: they are called Greco and Aglianico (or Ellenico), both of which mean Greek.

THE ROMANS AT WORK

The Romans generally worked very hard and, as this funerary relief
commemorating a well-known merchant shows, were proud of their
endeavours. It was possible for a freed slave to rise to a position of
great power and wealth, and within a generation or two for his
descendants to have scaled the highest ranks of government;
trade or a career in the army could provide such a fast track to success.

FROM SENATOR TO SLAVE

Knowing your place was most important in status-conscious Roman society.

But, despite the great gulf in wealth and privilege between rich and poor,

everyone was bound together in an intricate network of obedience and obligation.

IN ANCIENT ROME, great wealth was concentrated in the hands of a couple of hundred families. At the top of the social pyramid were the senators, with landed fortunes of at least a million sesterces (several hundred thousand times the daily wage of an ordinary labourer). Their social status, education and wealth made them eligible to command army legions, to be appointed to priesthoods and to act unpaid as the state's representatives in the major provinces. At the bottom of the pyramid were the slaves. And, in between senator and slave, there was an intricate system of property

qualification, personal merit, privilege and patronage separating the patricians from the plebeians.

Although most of his wealth came from the land, the wealthy Roman noble generally chose to live in the city, where he was duty-bound to throw himself into public life, scaling the heights of government.

LIFE AT THE TOP

The typical young man from the senatorial class gained his early experience as a lawyer. In his early thirties, he would hope to be elected for a one-year term to a magistracy such as that of quaestor

---

EYEWITNESS

'VULGAR AND UNSUITABLE FOR GENTLEMEN'

SENATORS could afford to look down on people who had to work for a living. In the 1st century BC, Marcus Tullius Cicero, elected quaestor at 31, aedile at 37, praetor at 40 and consul at 43, discussed a suitable job for a gentleman.

❛ We generally accept as true the following statements about trades and occupations, with regard to which are suitable for gentlemen and which are vulgar. First of all, those occupations are condemned which bring upon you people's hatred, such as tax collecting and usury. Also vulgar and unsuitable for gentlemen are the occupations of all hired workmen whom we pay for their labour, not for their artistic skills; for with these men, their

pay is itself a recompense for slavery. Also to be considered vulgar are retail merchants, who buy from wholesale merchants and immediately turn around and resell; for they would not make a profit unless they lied a lot. And nothing is more shameless than lying. All craftsmen, too, are engaged in vulgar occupations, for a workshop or factory can have nothing genteel about it. And the most shameful occupations are those which cater to our sensual pleasures....

However, occupations which involve a greater degree of intelligence or which provide no small service to society – such as medicine or architecture or teaching of liberal arts – these are proper for

men whose social position they suit. Trade, however, if it is small scale, must be considered vulgar; but if it is large scale, and involves importing many different items from throughout the world, and bringing many things to many people without lying or misrepresentation, it should not be greatly censured. Indeed it appears that large-scale trade could even be praised . . . if a man engaging in it . . . then moved from the harbour to a country estate, as he had often moved from the deep sea into a harbour. For, of all the occupations from which profit is accrued, none is better than agriculture, none more profitable, none more delightful, none more suitable to a free man. ❜

SENATE HOUSE Diocletian restored the Curia, the seat of the Roman Senate, in the 3rd century AD. A previous emperor (inset), Marcus Aurelius (AD 161-80), distributes money to poor Roman citizens.

'IN THIS TOWN NOBODY RAISES CHILDREN'

ROMANS devoted so much of their energies to the pursuit of wealthy legacies or wealthy heiresses that the subject became a common complaint of satirists in the 1st century AD. Here is a passage from the *Satyricon* by Petronius.

❛ In this town it's not the pursuit of one's studies that is talked about, eloquence has no standing, frugality and high morals don't produce the reward of praise.

No, any man you may see in this town, let me tell you, belongs to one of two classes, the legacy-hunters or the hunted. In this town nobody raises children. Whoever has his own heirs won't be asked to dinner parties or the theatre. He's locked out of the nice things, just stuck off in a corner among the no-accounts. But if he never married and has no clear relatives, he gets the top rank. ❜

(treasury official) – one of the major public offices. This would qualify him for lifelong admission to the Senate, which controlled the domestic and foreign affairs of Rome; during the Republic (509-27 BC) there were about 300 members at any one time. For the rest of his political career, he would continue to jockey for position and popularity, campaigning for ever more senior one-year magistracies. Above the quaestors came the aediles, who were responsible for public works; the consuls; the praetors, or senior judges; and most senior of all, during the Republic at least, the censors, ex-consuls who drew up the voting lists.

Politics at the highest level was a matter of connections: of making astute marriages and friendships with influential people. For many, therefore, the day consisted of an endless round of Senate meetings, jury duty, social functions and recitations. 'It's remarkable, isn't it,' complained Pliny the Younger, 'how you can offer a satisfactory account, or apparently satisfactory account, of your time in the city on any single day, but fail to make a satisfactory account of your time when you put all the days together. For if you ask someone, "What did you do today?" he will answer, "I went to a coming-of-age party; I attended an engagement party and then a wedding; one man asked me to be a witness at the signing of his will, another asked me for legal advice, a third asked me to sit in court . . .".'

A political career was also a matter of money. Wealthy Roman senators had to spend more and more just to match their predecessors and rivals. They staged spectacles in the arena and commissioned splendid public buildings, making sure that everyone was aware of their generosity – not difficult in a society where life was lived to such a large extent in the open. Some became victims of their own one-upmanship, contracting debts early in their careers which they could only repay later on, once they were administering a province, by imposing extortionate taxes on their Gallic, Spanish or Sicilian subjects. For example, a particularly unscrupulous governor of Sicily, Gaius Verres, was accused by the orator Cicero in 70 BC of using his position to amass a personal fortune of 40 million sesterces.

Although Roman senators hoped to manage their estates so successfully that they bequeathed to their heirs larger fortunes than they had inherited, they could still afford to despise people whose day-to-day jobs revolved around labour or commerce – in particular, successful freedmen, or ex-slaves, who had accumulated fortunes even greater than their own. However much they resisted getting

ELECTION TIME A Roman citizen drops his voting tablet into the ballot box; this system for electing magistrates was introduced in 139 BC.

SYMBOLS OF OFFICE
A magistrate's attendant, or lictor, carries a bundle of rods bound around an axe.

their own hands dirty, they prided themselves on being good and energetic managers. Their wealth was often shrewdly invested in a string of businesses, such as property speculation, mining, trade, manufacture, money-lending and tax collection, which were run by others, including their own freedmen or slaves, or was tied up in farms which, in their absence, were administered by stewards. In the 1st century BC there was even one aristocrat, Marcus Licinius Crassus, who increased his fortune by buying up houses for a knockdown price as they were actually on fire, and then arranging for his army of slave architects and builders to rebuild them hastily for resale.

It was the income from their land, together with their role as sleeping partners in other commercial interests, that allowed the senators to lead what they regarded as virtuous lives of active 'leisure', practising liberal professions, such as philosophy, oratory, law, poetry and medicine.

Towards the end of the 1st century BC, however, the absolute control that magistrates and members of the Senate had exerted over the city and its provinces was increasingly eroded by successive emperors. During the Republic, all male citizens had been allowed to vote in the election of government officials and on legislation which had been prepared beforehand by members of the Senate. However, in AD 14, the emperor Tiberius abolished popular elections – in Rome itself, ordinary citizens could no longer vote for a magistrate. Instead, magistrates were now often nominated by the emperor himself or replaced by career civil servants selected from the equestrian class.

After the senators, in ancient Rome's strict social hierarchy, came the knights, or members of the equestrian order. These people were generally wealthy businessmen with capital of at least 400 000 sesterces which, with interest rates of around 5 per cent, would provide an annual income of some 20 000 sesterces. They might be appointed as governor to minor provinces or to other senior administrative posts.

In a way that is surprising when viewed from a 20th-century perspective, practically every public function was a racket. Jobs that were theoretically unpaid were a source of income in the form of bribes; and it was regarded as perfectly acceptable for them to be bought and sold. It was also understood that official palms should be greased in order to get even the smallest favour done, and that people should pay their patrons for letters of recommendation to well-paid positions.

HIGH OFFICE
A toga-wearing consul of the late Republican period exudes all the dignity of his office.

Together, members of the senatorial and equestrian orders formed a ruling class, known as the *honestiores*, which accounted for less than 1 per cent of the population of the empire. They were separated from the rest of Rome's citizens, the *humiliores*, by a vast gulf in wealth and privileges: in the 2nd century AD, for example, the honestiores were exempted from punishments such as flogging, being burnt alive, thrown to wild beasts or crucified.

TRADERS AND TOWNSPEOPLE

Whatever the professed attitudes of the patrician towards wealth, the vast majority of Roman citizens worked hard for a living – and, as countless epitaphs show, were proud of it. Tombstones have been found showing a wealthy shopkeeper poring

---

THE MEDITERRANEAN UNION

In the 1st century AD, a Roman citizen could journey from the Near East to the border between England and Scotland without crossing a single foreign frontier. The Roman coins he carried were accepted everywhere along the route and he could get by with speaking only two languages – Greek between Mesopotamia and Yugoslavia, and Latin between Yugoslavia and Britain. Wherever he went, he was protected by Roman law.

MEAT TRADE In this open-fronted shop, a Roman butcher uses a cleaver to prepare cuts of pork, mutton and beef.

over his accounts; depicting the opulence of his shop's interior; or claiming that the deceased was a 'noted dealer in pork and beef' or a 'well-known money changer'. 'Long live profit', the words in a Pompeian mosaic, probably reflect most people's attitude – and everyone's behaviour – correctly.

The Romans had a real talent for business: indeed it was they who, recognising that commerce was a game of wits, bequeathed to posterity the phrase 'Let the buyer beware' (*Caveat emptor*). Traders followed in the wake of the conquering Roman legions, so that, during the heyday of ancient Rome, goods flooded into the city not only from the Italian countryside but also from every corner of the empire: tin from Roman Britain, wheat from North Africa, papyrus from Egypt, metals such as lead and silver from Spain, wood from Gaul, and glass from the Middle East; luxuries included amber from the Baltic, silks transported by caravan through central Asia from China, ivory from East Africa, and perfumes from Arabia. 'If anyone wants to see all these items,' wrote Aelius Aristides, a

'HE IS WELL BORN AND RICH'

IN A LETTER written between AD 103 and 107 that is typical of many such recommendations, Pliny the Younger implores Pompeius Falco to give his friend a job:

❝ You may have felt that I was rather pressing in my request for you to confer a military tribunate on a friend of mine, but you will be less surprised when you know who and what he is. Now that I have your promise I can give you his name and a full description. He is Cornelius Minicianus, in rank and character the pride of my native district.

He is well born and rich, but cares for literature as a poor professional might; and he is remarkable too for his justice on the bench, courage at the bar, and loyalty in friendship. You will feel that it is you who are receiving the favour when you come to know him more intimately and find that he is equal to any official position or distinction; I don't want to say more in praise of the most modest of men. ❞

Greek rhetorician of the 2nd century AD, 'he must either travel through the whole world to behold them, or live in this city.' He was referring to Rome where, day in and day out, dockers unloaded goods into warehouses on the banks of the Tiber or on the slopes of the Aventine Hill.

In most towns, people who plied the same trade clustered together in particular areas. So, for example, a Roman's address might have been Perfume Street or, when asked where he lived, he might have replied 'among the butchers'. In Pompeii, the cloth trade – dyers, fullers and combers – were concentrated in the Via dell'Abbondanza; and in all cities, carters quite naturally congregated around the gates ready to transport visitors out of town in their wagons. The main reason for this grouping was so that buyers would know exactly where to find what they wanted – or, in the case of tanners, to confine an industry whose stench was particularly noxious to out-of-the way areas of the town.

Painted boards were set up outside shops to attract people's attention, and goods often spilled out onto the pavements – exacerbating the congestion. In Rome, the great Forum was the main business centre, with a huge complex of shops, money-changers' stalls, market squares and meeting places. By AD 300, there were 2300 sellers of olive oil alone in Rome – oil was used for cooking, burnt in lamps and was sometimes used, rather like soap, for washing the body.

Because of the crowded conditions in which they lived and worked, and the fact that most of the day was spent outside in the streets, the Romans had a great sense of local community and a pride in their chosen trade. Most craftsmen paid an initiation fee and then monthly dues to belong to a trade association. As well as butchers

HARVEST TIME **In this mosaic from northern Africa, a peasant gathers fruit in the autumn.**

and bakers, there were the cobblers and carpenters, farriers, florists and floor-layers, mosaicists and millhands, and so on. In a typically Roman search for status, they gave their groups grand-sounding names, the Most August Union of Fishers, for example, or the Corporation of Most Noble Money-changers. Every now and then, these trade associations agitated in defence of their economic interests – the repeal of a tax on salt for use in bleaching, say – but, in general, their purpose was purely social. They sought the patronage of a wealthy person who might build them a meeting-place; they prayed together to an appropriate god (restaurateurs chose Bacchus, for example); they tried to have their own festivals added to the city's official calendar; they petitioned for blocks of seats in the amphitheatre to be reserved for their exclusive use; they paid the funeral expenses of members; and they held group banquets at which everyone was expected to enjoy himself. According to the constitution of a provincial Italian association, 'if anyone wishes to bring up any matter of complaint he shall do so in a business meeting, so that our dinners on the usual days may pass off serenely and joyfully'.

LIFE ON THE LAND

Although craftsmen and traders could make a good living, any of the free poor lived at subsistence level – particularly those 90 per cent of the empire's population who lived on the land. 'Happy is the man who remains far from business and cultivates the family farm with his own oxen', wrote the poet Horace, a lover of life's good things.

DUCK HUNT **A peasant chases a couple of ducks – a delicacy of the Roman table.**

'WHY, WHAT WAS WRONG WITH ME?'

MOST SLAVES looked forward to the possibility of freedom, and the opportunity to advance themselves – as many freedmen had done before them. However, as the Stoic philosopher and former slave Epictetus described in the 1st century AD, life as a freedman could be just as harsh.

❛ Then he is emancipated, and forthwith, having no place to which to go and eat, he looks for someone to flatter, for someone at whose house to dine.

Next he either earns a living by prostitution, and so endures the most dreadful of things, and if he gets a manger at which to eat he has fallen into a slavery much more than the first; or even if he grows rich, being a vulgarian he has fallen in love with a chit of a girl, and is miserable, and laments, and yearns for his slavery again.

"Why, what was wrong with me? Someone else kept me in clothes, and shoes, and supplied me with food, and nursed me when I was sick; I served him in only a few matters. But now, miserable man that I am, what suffering is mine, who am a slave to several instead of one!" ❜

But, despite the romantic notions about rural life preached by many writers, much of the Mediterranean soil was poor and rainfall low. Local shortages of food – and even famine – were common in the countryside.

Small independent farmers struggled to pay their taxes, the collection of which the imperial government left to local notables, who gradually squeezed them out and acquired their land. The lot of many tenant farmers, sharecroppers (who paid the landowner a share of their harvest) and free agricultural labourers, who moved around the country, hiring themselves out for seasonal work, such as harvesting, ditch-digging and cutting hay, cannot have been much better than that of the slaves.

As land ownership became increasingly concentrated in the hands of a few, many peasant farmers were forced to move to the towns: a sad fate for the sturdy descendants of those soldiers who had turned a tiny village beside the Tiber into the centre of an empire stretching from Spain to Syria. In the towns, many of the free poor – working as porters, say, or alongside slaves in bakeries or pottery factories – depended on public or private charity.

THE REWARDS OF RESPECT

The first task of a typical Roman male's day was to pay his respects at the home of his patron (everyone but the most powerful of all was someone's client). The *salutatio*, or 'morning salute', was part of the chain of respect that held the Roman social system together – from the ex-slave to the master who had freed him.

The client would arrive at his patron's home, and line up in order of rank before being admitted into the antechamber to ask for his help in legal and business matters. He would also collect a parcel of food or, as became increasingly the practice, a cash gift – around 6 1/4 sesterces per person in the time of the emperor Trajan (AD 98-117). Favoured clients might be invited to

WINE BARGE
Labourers use ropes to haul a barge transporting wine barrels along the waterways of Europe.

dine with their patrons from time to time, if only to be ostentatiously insulted by his servants, and they might also hope to benefit from their patrons' wills.

In return, the patron would expect his client to flatter him, to support his political campaigns (particularly during the Republic) and generally to advertise what a powerful man he was. Poorer Romans tried to ingratiate themselves with as many patrons as possible in order to multiply their takings. And the poorest of all – around 150 000 citizens in Rome's imperial heyday – queued at the portico of Minucius to collect the wooden tablet which they later exchanged for their monthly dole of free grain and, later, free bread.

IRONMONGER This tomb shows the freedman Cornelius Atimetus dressed in a tunic (right) selling knives to a customer wearing a toga.

THE LIFE OF THE SLAVE

Slaves provided much of the muscle power in everyday life. After the Republican wars of expansion which began in the 3rd century BC, hundreds of thousands of captured people were brought to Italy from the Mediterranean world to work as slaves on

farms, in mines, grain mills or homes. Their numbers were swelled by poverty-stricken families who sometimes sold their children, or even themselves, into slavery – to be bought like animals at public auction, with placards around their necks advertising their merits and make-up on their faces disguising an unhealthy complexion. In time, this domestic slave population multiplied, so that by the 1st century AD, around a quarter of the people in Italy and a third of the population of Rome were slaves.

Many of the empire's most miserable jobs, such as collecting rubbish, mining (which had a particularly high mortality rate) and turning grindstones, were reserved for slaves. 'Good gods,' observed the Roman writer Apuleius of a grain mill in the 2nd century AD, 'what scrawny little slaves they were! Their skin was everywhere embroidered with purple welts from their many beatings. Their backs, scarred from many floggings, were shaded, as it were, rather than actually covered by their torn patchwork garments. Some wore only flimsy loincloths. All of them, decked out in these rags, carried brands on their foreheads, had their heads half-shaved, and wore chains around their ankles. Their complexions were an ugly yellow; their eyes were so inflamed by the thick dark smoke and the steamy vapour that they could barely see.'

The harsh treatment of many slaves was partly

IDENTITY BADGE The inscription on this bronze slave-tag directs the reader to return the escaped slave to his master.

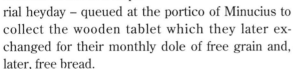

TRAVEL TIPS

The Romans were a superstitious people – particularly when it came to travel. Ships would not set sail on August 24, October 5 or November 8, the traditional days of entry into the underworld. A sneeze on the gangplank, a glimpse of a magpie in the rigging, or a bad dream the night before (especially if it featured goats, wild boars, bulls or owls) were all poor omens. However, if the weather deteriorated during the course of the voyage, you could always throw some nail clippings or locks of hair into the sea to appease the gods.

TRAJAN'S COLUMN: THE DACIAN WARS IN MARBLE

ON MAY 13, AD 113 Emperor Trajan inaugurated a marble column, designed by the great architect Apollodorus of Damascus, in the heart of the imperial city. As an inscription above the door at the base records, the column, 130 ft (40 m) tall, was erected by the Senate and people of Rome to mark the height of a hill that had previously stood on that

VICTORY COLUMN The emperor Trajan inaugurated his column 130 ft (40 m) high in AD 113 to celebrate his victorious campaigns in Dacia, present-day Romania.

spot and had been excavated to make way for Trajan's magnificent forum – the last and largest of all the Roman forums. The column was a triumph over nature. But more specifically, as the series of marble reliefs which spiral up the shaft of the column reveal, it also commemorated Trajan's victory over a barbarian people.

In AD 101 Trajan had gone to war with the Dacians, who lived north of the Danube in what is now Romania. After two bruising and bloody campaigns (AD 101-102 and AD 105-106), Trajan routed the Dacians under their leader Decebalus. Dacia became a Roman province, and vast amounts of captured gold and silver were brought back to Rome to swell the treasury and to finance ambitious building projects in the city.

From the ground, it is quite difficult now to identify all the scenes portrayed in the continuous frieze of 23 marble panels which, if unrolled and spread flat, would measure almost 600 ft (200 m). But they would originally have been viewed from upper-floor galleries in the buildings around the column. The reliefs chronicle the course of the wars, from the Roman army first crossing the Danube to the besieged Dacian leaders committing collective

WAR STORY The marble friezes that spiral around the column tell the story of the military campaigns.

suicide around a cauldron containing poison. They also provide a very precise record of life in the Roman army: the everyday routines of felling trees and collecting wood, reaping corn and attending sacrifices. Altogether, some 2500 figures are represented, with Trajan himself appearing 60 times. In order to promote himself as a fair leader, after the tyrannies of Emperor Domitian, Trajan is portrayed on the column as a compassionate general. He shares the hardships of war with his soldiers, and is not shown as a cruel oppressor of the people he has conquered.

Trajan died in AD 117, and his ashes were brought back to Rome from Asia and placed in a golden urn in the pedestal of the column.

GRAIN CARGO   In this wall-painting, a merchant ship of the 2nd or 3rd century AD is being loaded with grain.

because their masters were actually frightened of them. 'No master can feel safe because he is kind and considerate', wrote Pliny the Younger on hearing of the bathtime murder by his slaves of the 'cruel and overbearing' senator Larcius Macedo. In another case, when a city official called Pedanius Secundus was murdered in AD 61 by one of his slaves, all 400 of them were executed. There are also instances of slave revolts – two in Sicily in the 2nd century BC and the third, consisting of 90 000 slaves led by the gladiator Spartacus, in Italy itself in 73 BC.

In the words of a Roman proverb, the number of one's enemies equalled the number of one's slaves. As a result, the slaves were kept under constant supervision to curb what were believed to be their naturally idle and criminal tendencies. Troublesome slaves were kept in chains, and some owners forced their slaves to wear iron collars with instructions on where they should be returned if they ran away. 'I have run away,' ran the inscription on one. 'Capture me. When you have returned me to my master, Zoninus, you will receive a reward.'

Despite laws in the 1st and 2nd centuries AD to prevent masters from committing the worst excesses, such as castration or cold-blooded murder, slaves often faced ferocious punishments if they displeased. These included branding (for runaway slaves), flogging (as many as 300 lashes for taking too long to bring hot water, according to one commentator), and tortures so sadistic that they must have tested even the Romans' ingenuity. Vedius Pollio, an equestrian and friend of the emperor Augustus, is said to have thrown a boy who had broken a crystal cup to man-eating eels. And the historian Suetonius records how the emperor Caligula ordered the hands of a slave who had stolen a strip of silver from a couch to be hacked off and tied around his neck; he was then paraded around the tables with a placard explaining his punishment. There was nothing a slave could do about such treatment if it was ordered by the emperor, and very little if he received it from his own master. In theory, he could complain to the city prefect but in practice, he was unlikely to receive a sympathetic hearing from yet another member of the ruling class. As a consequence, slaves were generally so cowed by their masters' enforcement of servile obedience that they behaved with the docility expected of them; even the Christians instructed servants to obey their masters in this life, leaving the notion of equality for the life to come.

CATERING TO THE RICH At a lavish Roman banquet, slaves attend to every need of the wealthy diners.

However, the lot of the slave was not always so bad. Slaves in towns generally fared better than those put to work in the fields or worked to death in the lead, copper, iron or silver mines. Although subject to the sexual attentions of predatory owners, household slaves were often treated with real affection by the families they served – as can be seen in funerary inscriptions expressing the grief of a master for a deceased slave. They might become doctors, estate managers, teachers and, in some cases, government officials – positions in which they were treated much like free men. The imperial household, for example, consisted of up to 20 000 slaves in different locations, numbering cooks, hairdressers, cupbearers and clothes attendants among its ranks. It also included a civil service composed, to a large extent, of slaves processing petitions and relaying the instructions of the emperor.

Owners used the carrot as well as the stick; and this made the life of many slaves less intolerable.

TRAVELLING THE HIGHWAYS OF EMPIRE

AT ITS HEIGHT, the Roman Empire stretched from Hadrian's Wall in the north to the edge of the Sahara in the south, and from Spain in the west to Syria in the east. Knitting together these far-flung provinces was a network of highways that eventually stretched for over 50 000 miles (80 000 km), and laid the basis for many of today's roads and railway lines.

Most of these roads were built by and for the Roman army, connecting military camps and towns. But traders soon followed in the soldiers' wake. Laden with farm produce, their carts ploughed deep furrows in the paving stones and competed with government officers, such as judges and district officials, for right of way. Some ordinary citizens on private business travelled on foot or muleback. Others hired two-wheeled cabs or four-wheeled wagons, pulled by mules or horses,

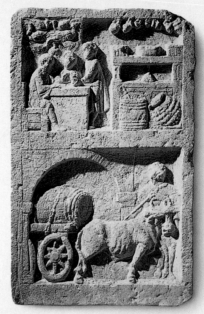

WINE TRADE A funerary relief shows a tavern scene (top) and the transportation of wine (below).

from the rental firms found in every sizable town. And the very rich travelled in litters carried by up to eight slaves.

Every mile, or thousand five-foot paces (*mille* is Latin for a thousand), there was a milestone, which gave the distance from Rome or from the city where the road had started. Every 10 miles (16 km) or so, there was a post station where relays of horse-riders passed on official government communications and where, on the presentation of a diploma or warrant, officials on government business could change their horses and have a meal. And, finally, every 30 miles (48 km) there were government-controlled guesthouses, all of them listed in maps or itineraries. Priority for beds was given to officials, although members of the public could pay for the facilities, which included meals, a bed and the services of a vet or cartwright. Alternatively, you could put up in a simple inn and risk the bedbugs, indifferent food and loutish behaviour of some of the other guests.

People on foot averaged up to 20 miles (32 km) a day, carriages around 30, and government dispatch riders up to 50 miles (80 km). However, in emergencies, such as the mutiny on the Rhine in AD 69, government couriers relayed the news at the rate of more than 150 miles (240 km) per day.

In spring, the leisured classes retreated to villas in the cool hill country around Rome or beside the sea in the Bay of Naples – in such numbers that the poet Horace complained that even the fish were feeling cramped. It was not unusual, then, to see whole households on the move from town to country, with their bedding, changes of clothing, kitchen equipment and provisions of food and drink.

RUTTED ROAD Ruts cut into roads made travel easier for wheeled vehicles.

Freighters of the Mediterranean

In the 1st and 2nd centuries AD, the Mediterranean world was more united than it ever has been before or since and had more merchant ships at its disposal than all the countries of Europe had put together until the 18th century.

Hundreds of ships crisscrossed the sea between Rome, Marseilles, Narbonne, Tarragona, Cartagena, Alexandria, Cadiz, Caesarea, Arles, Antioch and Carthage, transporting wine from France, olive oil from Spain and 150 000 tons of wheat a year from Egypt.

With its large round hull, big square mainsail, small triangular topsail and its squaresail at the prow, the typical cargo ship was not designed for speed. But it was sturdy enough, and the largest vessels, which were more than 180 ft (55 m) long and 45 ft (14 m) wide, could hold around 1000 tons of grain as well as several hundred passengers. Despite an average speed of only three and a half knots (6.5 km/h), a ship might take as little as ten days to travel from Italy to Egypt (the return journey against the summer trade winds might take as much as two months). Although the ships were designed principally for cargo, passengers could pick up vessels at the waterfront, and take their own servants, supplies, pots, pans and bedding on board with them, sleeping on deck.

Travelling by sea was a risky business. There was always the danger of attack by pirates particularly off the coast of North Africa. But the traveller's worst enemies were storms and cloudy weather, which made navigation by the sun and stars almost impossible between November and March.

IMPERIAL PORT A mosaic in Ostia shows a couple of merchant ships beside the lighthouse of the Port of Claudius.

According to the Roman agricultural writer Columella, slaves were to be clothed properly, allowed to bathe every now and then, treated when sick, and consulted occasionally by their masters. But, despite the apparent humanitarianism of these recommendations, their intention was practical: to make the slaves more productive. For the same reason, slave-owners used a variety of incentives to foster a sense of loyalty and obedience on the part of their slaves.

They were given holidays on certain festivals, including the *Matronalia* on March 1, *Fors Fortuna* on June 24, the *Saturnalia* in December when masters served their slaves with special meals rather than the other way round, and the *Compitalia* in January. Slaves were also allowed some sort of family life – particularly those serving in the wealthy households of the capital. Many masters turned a blind eye to the Roman law which, until about AD 200, prevented slaves from marrying, and permitted their slaves to raise families; indeed, it was often in the owners' interests to maintain the slave population by encouraging breeding.

These families, however, could be disrupted at the whim of the master: as the owner's property, individual slaves could be sold and transported hundreds of miles from their place of birth, bequeathed in wills, loaned, handed over as part of a dowry, or simply given away – regardless of their own family circumstances. It was only when each member had been emancipated individually that the ex-slave family could function without fear of separation; and it is hardly surprising that, in conditions of such uncertainty, most slaves attempted to protect what little comfort and security they had by acquiescence.

For a few slaves, mostly domestic servants in the city who regularly came into close contact with their masters, there was always the tantalising prospect of eventual emancipation. Some were quite simply rewarded with freedom for their loyal service. Others had to buy their liberty with personal savings from tips and wages (as well, sometimes, as paying the government tax on emancipation). Master and slave would then appear

MAKING A SLAVE OF YOUR PARENT

There are cases in Roman history of a child being freed from slavery before his parents and then purchasing his parents from their owner. In these cases, the parents, until set free, became the slaves of the child. This was a reversal of the more normal procedure. Any children born after a slave parent had been freed were automatically considered as having been born free. Children born before their parents had been freed, however, were born into slavery and remained the property of the master, until their parents were emancipated and purchased their children's freedom.

before a magistrate – a praetor in Rome or a proconsul in the provinces – who would formally confer freedom on the slave with a touch of a rod or wand.

The freed slave still owed his former master a form of homage known as *obsequium* (from which, our word 'obsequious'). He had to support him in public life and to give him a certain number of days of work a year (which offset, to an extent, the owner's financial loss in granting the freedom). Some masters had their favourite slaves train as poets or accountants, or even practise as prostitutes, and then hired them out, allowing them to save some of their earnings in order eventually to buy their freedom. What the owners hoped to gain from freeing slaves was some respect from their peers for their apparent generosity; and many of them postponed this glorious, but expensive, moment until their deathbeds (Pliny the Younger, for example, freed around 100 of his 500 slaves in his will).

Once a slave had been freed, however, he did not qualify immediately for the rights of full citizenship. There was a half-way house, where freed slaves could not, for example, vote, run for public office, benefit from wills or, indeed, make wills of their own. Laws passed during the reign of the emperor Augustus stipulated that the freed slave had to be over 30 to qualify for citizenship (an achievement, in itself, since this was the average life expectancy); and that citizenship was not to be granted to freed slaves 'who had ever been put in irons or tortured', branded or fought as a gladiator. These restrictions ensured that the slave had to earn his citizenship by many years of obedience and good behaviour.

Most freed slaves set up as shopkeepers, traders and merchants. Some became extremely rich, like the fictitious Trimalchio, the vulgar hero of Petronius's *Satyricon* whose fortune was put at around 30 million sesterces. Although accounting for as little as 5 per cent of the population, these freedmen formed a particularly dynamic and upwardly mobile sector of society – and many senators were the grandsons of ex-slaves. With its dwindling population, the emancipation of slaves – or 'manumission', as it was called – was essential to Roman society. The ranks of the citizenry required constant transfusions of new blood – which slaves from all corners of the Roman Empire provided.

THE ARMY CAMP

WHEN on campaign, the Romans built camps that were to serve as models for their frontier forts and even for many towns in the provinces. Surveyors were sent ahead to select well-drained sites, preferably beside a river, and plan the layout, placing the commander's tent (*praetorium*) and the headquarters (*principia*) in the middle, facing towards the enemy. Two axes – the *via principalis* and the *via praetoria* – met at a T-junction in an open area by the commander's tent. Leather tents, each sleeping eight men, were arranged in lines around the centre. Defences consisted of a ditch encircling the camp; earth from the ditch was then piled into a bank on which the soldiers planted the stakes they carried to form a palisade. The main features of many Roman forts were derived from such marching camps.

Praetorium
(commander's tent)

Principia
(headquarters)

Rubbish pit

Rampart,
built to regulation
height and turfed

Palisade

Digging a ditch

Drill area

Watchtowers

Ablution tents

Troops exercise by marching

LIFE IN THE ARMY

From a part-time fighting force, the Roman army developed into a

highly trained professional organisation, where an ordinary citizen

could forge a successful lifetime's career.

IN THE HEYDAY of the empire during the 1st and 2nd centuries AD, the Roman army was a devastating war machine the like of which the world had never seen. From the shores of Galilee to the moors of northern England, its soldiers secured a vast empire, encompassing 60 million people. During the early days of the Republic, however, there had been no standing army in Rome. In those days, the Roman army had existed only

when the city was at war. When the trumpets sounded and the red flags were flown around the city, all able-bodied, property-owning citizens between the ages of 17 and 46 reported for duty on the Field of Mars (named after the god of war). The soldiers were then selected, made to take an oath of loyalty to their general, and instructed to assemble on a particular day at a military camp near the action. Under Julius Caesar in the 1st century BC,

EYEWITNESS

'HE PRAISED THE SOLDIERS WHO HAD SERVED UNDER HIM'

THE EMPEROR Augustus and his successors reserved the honour of a triumph to themselves. However, during the Republic, the city had honoured successful generals in this way. The description below was written in the Middle Ages by a historian called Zonaras, and based on the lost writings of the Roman historian Dio Cassius:

❝ Dressed in triumphal garb and wearing bracelets on his arms and a crown of laurel on his head, and holding a branch in his right hand, he [the triumphant general] summoned the people together. Then he praised the soldiers who had served under him, both collectively and, in some cases, individually, and made them gifts of money and honoured them also with military decorations, presenting arm bracelets to some and spears (but without

iron tips) to others, crowns – some gold, some silver – each crown bearing the name of the honoured individual and a representation of his particular brave deed . . . When these ceremonies had been completed, the triumphant general mounted his chariot . . . At the head of the procession were the spills and trophies, placards bearing representations of captured forts, cities, mountains, rivers, lakes and seas, indeed all the things they had captured. And if one day was sufficient for the exhibition of these things, fine. If not, the exhibition continued for a second or even third day. When all the men ahead of him had reached the concluding point

of the procession, the general [who was at the end of the procession] finally was escorted into the Roman Forum. He ordered some of the captives to be led to prison and executed, and then he drove up to the Capitol. ❞

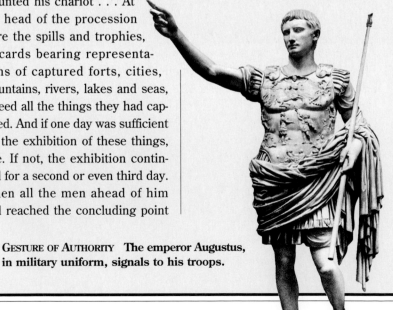

GESTURE OF AUTHORITY The emperor Augustus, in military uniform, signals to his troops.

ON PARADE Infantrymen and foot soldiers on parade around the base of the Column of Antoninus Pius.

the army became an increasingly efficient organisation and, by the end of the reign of the emperor Augustus, it was completely professional – a permanent army for peacetime as well as war.

ARMY ORGANISATION

The highly paid praetorian guard – an elite corps which formed the emperor's bodyguard – was stationed around Rome. The empire's main fighting force, however, was represented by the 28 or so legions, each consisting of around 5000 men, mostly infantry soldiers, who were deployed in frontier areas. Each legion was divided into ten cohorts, and each cohort into six 'centuries' of around 80 soldiers apiece (led by a centurion) – the basic fighting unit of the legion. The Romans were not great horse riders, and when they did raise cavalry regiments they generally employed foreign auxiliaries, among them Gauls and Thracians, who might be rewarded with Roman citizenship at the end of their period of service. Other auxiliaries –

fighters recruited from all over the empire for their specialist skills – included archers, javelin throwers and slingers. Last but not least, there was the Roman navy. During the Civil War of the 1st century BC, around 1000 ships had been active in the Mediterranean, and the importance of seapower was not lost on the emperor Augustus who set about building a professional navy. Although it was always considered very much a junior service under army control, the navy soon consisted of fleets at Misenum and Ravenna on the Italian coast, with smaller forces in the Eastern Mediterranean and on the Danube, Rhine and Black Sea.

JOINING THE PROFESSIONALS

As the armed forces became more professional, the army became a career option for the prospective soldier – rather than simply the unpaid annual obligation of the citizen. The legionary would enlist for a period of 20 years, with a further five years' service as a veteran. Armed with a letter of recommendation,

BATTLE SCENE **Roman legionaries engage in fierce hand-to-hand fighting with barbarian soldiers in this tomb relief.**

volunteers would report for an interview and medical examination. Young recruits had to be Roman citizens, over 5 ft 8 in (1.7 m) tall and, according to the author Vegetius, writing in the 4th century AD, 'ought to have alert eyes, should carry his head erect, have a broad chest, muscular shoulders, strong arms, long fingers, a small waist, slim buttocks, and legs and feet which are not fleshy but sinewy and strong'.

If selected, the soldier would then take an oath of loyalty and obedience, receive an advance of 75 denarii on his wages, and be posted to a particular unit to which he would travel in the company of his fellow recruits. On arrival, he was allocated to a particular century and began basic training in the barracks: parade-ground drill, marching, and exercises such as swimming or vaulting over a wooden horse. Recruits trained at first with double-weight practice weapons – lunging at 6 ft (1.8 m) high wooden stakes with their shield and sword. Training in the field consisted of instruction in battle formations, practice at building camps, and route marches – at the rate of almost 5 miles (8 km) an hour carrying equipment that weighed over 66 lb (30 kg), which is more than most modern soldiers have to bear.

Training camps could be extremely arduous: according to the Roman historian Tacitus, one winter during Nero's reign was so severe that, under the command of a particularly tough general called Corbulo, 'many men suffered from frostbite, and one or two men were frozen to death while on guard. A case was reported of a soldier who was carrying a bundle of logs; his hands were frozen so hard that they became fastened to his load and fell off from the stumps of his arms.'

Punishments were famously severe, too. In the event of a mutiny, every tenth man in a rebellious cohort was chosen by lot to be beaten or stoned to death by his fellows – a practice known as decimation (from the Latin *decimus*, meaning 'tenth'). The remaining nine-tenths might have their rations of wheat replaced by barley. Individual deserters were executed or flogged, while other punishments included fines, extra fatigues, demotion and dishonourable discharges. Not even officers were exempt: according to the historian Suetonius, the emperor Augustus humiliated disobedient centurions by making them 'stand all day in front of the general's headquarters sometimes clad only in their tunics and without sword-belts, or sometimes holding a ten-foot pole or even a piece of earth'.

ARMS, ARMOUR AND THE ART OF WARFARE

SOME HISTORIANS have suggested that the Roman soldier on the march during a campaign had to carry more equipment than any soldier in history before World War I. The soldier's basic clothing was light enough, however: a short-sleeved, knee-length woollen tunic over a linen undergarment, with hobnailed boots on his feet. In the colder parts of the Roman Empire, he might also wear a hooded cloak, calf-length leather trousers, and fleeces or fur strapped to the shin by leather thongs. Senior officers and centurions were distinguished by cloaks made of much finer material, decorated belts and the greaves they wore on their shins.

But the weight of the armour, made of metal plates and strips, more than made up for the

BACK PACK Soldiers carried both rations and weapons on their back.

HUMAN SHIELD Soldiers use their shields to form a *testudo,* or protective tortoise-like shell.

flimsiness of the clothing. On his head, a legionary wore an iron or bronze helmet with a piece that curved out at the back to protect the neck, a ridge in front to shield the face, and cheek-pieces at the sides. Every legionary had a wooden shield covered in leather and studded with bronze decorations, two 7 ft (2 m) javelins, a double-edged sword for the cut and thrust of close combat, and a dagger fastened to his belt. As if this was not enough to carry, there were also his food rations and tools for building defences: a saw, a basket for moving earth, a pickaxe, and a couple of staves for the palisade. At least he did not have to carry the millstones for grinding corn: these were borne by mules.

Romans were as impressive in siege warfare as they were on the field of battle. To take city gates, a group of 27 legionaries would pack themselves tightly into a *testudo* or tortoise formation, holding their shields overhead to create a 'shell' of armour against enemy missiles. They also used battering rams, which they concealed in mobile sheds covered with animal hides and iron plates; wooden towers, which they assembled alongside the enemy fortifications and from which they could fire down on the defenders or even storm across on drawbridges; and catapults which hurled boulders, beams and firebrands. According to the historian Josephus, describing the siege of Jerusalem, some of these were capable of throwing 55 lb (25 kg) boulders 440 yards (402 m). If all these weapons failed, the Romans – exhibiting that mixture of practical genius and patience that characterised so many of their activities – simply constructed a ring of defences around the besieged area to cut the defenders off from any supplies or reinforcements.

BLADE BEAUTY A legionary's sword and sheath from the 1st century AD.

Given such harsh conditions and horrendous punishments, why did the average soldier volunteer? Many were attracted by the wages – around 225 denarii a year for the ordinary legionary, less stoppages for food and clothes. Any savings he made from this annual income was deposited in the legion's savings bank. This was supplemented by extra payments, or donatives, authorised by the emperor, who was also the commander-in-chief of the army, to mark special occasions and to buy the personal loyalty of his men. And finally there was the lure of a large payment on retirement. The emperor Augustus had rewarded his veterans by granting them land in a series of settlements he established around Italy, but this practice was gradually replaced by gifts of money – around 3000 denarii after 20 years' service.

There was also always the prospect of advancement. For a start, specialists such as surveyors, clerks and medical orderlies were exempt from general duties. Along with the other legionaries, they might seek promotion to the ranks of the Roman equivalent of the noncommissioned officers, or *principales*, such as standard-bearer and quartermaster. Eventually they might reach the rank of centurion – most of whom had begun their careers in the ranks. With these ranks went higher wages – around 400 denarii a year for the principales and 4500 denarii in the 2nd century AD for the centurion. Centurions might be posted from legion to legion around the Roman Empire until they reached the rank of senior centurion.

The most senior officers were not necessarily career soldiers, however, and many would have been far less experienced than the centurions who actually led the men in battle. The military tribunes were generally young men of equestrian rank with administrative jobs rather than the responsibilities of

IMPERIAL ADDRESS   Carved on the Arch of
Constantine, the emperor addresses his troops.

direct command; the senior tribune came from the senatorial class and saw his appointment as a steppingstone to a political career in the Senate; and the general was a full senator, who would move on to other administrative duties after his four-year spell in command of the legion.

INTO BATTLE WITH THE LEGIONS

Since no military manuals from ancient Rome have survived in their entirety, the only way in which historians are able to reconstruct the tactics of a typical battle is by comparing contemporary accounts of the skirmishes themselves.

The night before an engagement, the soldiers were fed their staple campaign diet of hard cornmeal biscuits and wine, and were encouraged to get plenty of rest. At break of dawn the following day, the general addressed his troops in an open area beside his tent, stirring his men into a rage against the enemy; so that, by the time they were ready for battle, they added their bloodcurdling cries to the cacophony of trumpet blasts communicating orders. With the sun and the wind behind them to blind their opponents and to whip the dust into their eyes, the legionaries trotted down the slope towards the enemy

T·FLAVIS·BASSVS·MVCALAE
F·DANSALA·EQ·ALAE·NOR
CORV·TVR·FABI·PVDENTIS
AN·XXXXVI·STP·XXVI·H·F·C

58

AT THE KILL   According to the inscription, a Roman cavalryman, Flavius Bassus, rides down a barbarian soldier.

lines. Leading the troops was the strange figure of the standard-bearer, dressed in animal skins and carrying the eagle that acted as a rallying-point for the legion, and the loss of which would have been the ultimate disgrace.

The soldiers marched in ranks, with about 3 ft (1 m) on either side of each man and some 6 ft (1.8 m) in front and behind. As soon as they spotted a weakness in the enemy line, a small group of them surged forwards to drive a wedge into it. Meanwhile, the cavalry waited in the wings to prevent the footsoldiers in the centre from being outflanked and to charge the enemy as soon as

CIVIL RIGHTS A bronze diploma, dated AD 103, confers rights of citizenship and marriage upon a Spaniard who has retired after 25 years in the army.

they started to retreat. One of the reasons why these tactics were so supremely successful was that they were pursued with such discipline. In AD 77, the Jewish historian Flavius Josephus, who had been a prisoner of war of the Romans, recorded the awesome resolve of the Roman legionary: 'Their perfect discipline welds the whole into a single body; so compact are their ranks, so alert their movements in wheeling, so quick their ears for orders, their eyes for signals, their hands for tasks.'

Despite the warlike reputation of the Roman army, the constant frontier skirmishing involved only relatively small numbers of men, and many legionary soldiers may never have seen active service on campaign. Instead, the army's role was to preserve the 'Roman peace', or *Pax Romana*. With its well-organised contingents of skilled architects, surveyors and engineers, the army got involved in public works, building roads, bridges and aqueducts, which encouraged trade and commerce. It

FRONTIER FORT   In this aerial view of Housesteads Roman Fort in the North of England, the military headquarters are clearly visible in the centre, with two barrack-blocks in the top right, and the remains of the civilian settlement outside the fort walls.

ACCOUNTS FROM A ROMAN FORT

IN 1973 more than 200 wooden writing tablets were discovered at the Roman fort of Vindolanda in northern Britain. Dating from around AD 100, they have enabled historians to reconstruct not only the way in which ancient Romans wrote but also the day-to-day activities of life in a fort. For example, a daily account of food supplies refers to barley, Celtic beer, wine, fish-sauce, salt, spices, wheat, and meats such as ham, pork, and venison. Employment records show that some of the soldiers were detailed to the workshops, while others were building a bathhouse and a

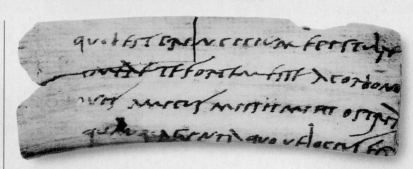

THANKYOU LETTER In a letter from Vindolanda, inscribed on a wooden writing tablet, a decurion called Lucius records a gift of 50 oysters.

hospital. A letter of recommendation asks Flavius Cerialis, the fort's commander, to further the career of one Brigonius. And, on an even more mundane level, a letter to one of the auxiliary soldiers stationed at Vindolanda, probably from a relative notes: 'I have sent you . . . pairs of socks . . . two pairs of sandals and two pairs of underpants.'

also acted as a police force, guarding mines or offering protection to civilian administrators.

Soldiers were posted to frontier forts for long periods of time, and tended to settle down. Although the law prevented them from marrying, the army turned a blind eye to unofficial marriages with local women: such arrangements made the soldiers happier and any sons, although technically illegitimate, were potential recruits. Settlements grew up around the forts, consisting of traders and the families of serving soldiers. On retirement, many veterans simply moved from the fort into the civilian settlement and lived with their families, sharing in the life of the community and even adopting some of the local gods in addition to the official cults of Jupiter, Juno, Minerva, Mars and Victory recognised by the Roman army.

Like many an army of occupation, the Roman legions often bullied the local civilian population, requisitioning more or less anything they wanted. But overall it was this peaceful and productive involvement in local projects and in local lifestyles that transformed the Roman army into something more than a merely military force: that made it the standard-bearer of Roman civilisation.

PRISONER OF WAR In a scene from the Arch of Constantine, a Roman soldier escorts his prisoner.

THE ROMANS AT PLAY

Charioteers career around the Circus Maximus under the
watchful eyes of statues of the gods in whose honour the games
were held. Other popular leisure activities included the theatre,
visits to the Roman baths and gladiator fights in the
amphitheatre where, according to the philosopher Seneca,
'all niceties were put aside and it was pure and simple murder'.

THE LEISURED SOCIETY

Hard though the Romans worked, they were rewarded with

hours of spare time in which to game, gamble and gossip,

and with a plethora of public holidays.

LEISURE WAS part of daily life in ancient Rome, and the calendar was packed with public holidays, or *feriae*, and days reserved for public games, or *ludi*. Coining a phrase that was to become one of the most famous Latin tags of all, the poet Juvenal complained that the Roman people had become 'eager and anxious for two things only: bread and circuses'. He was referring to the distributions of free grain and bread to the inhabitants of Rome, and to the way in which the state occupied the leisure hours of its citizens by providing at public expense an array of shows and spectacles. In imperial times, adding in the days set aside as holidays in honour of the emperors' birthdays and their great military ventures, Romans enjoyed a staggering total of 159 days of public holiday a year (a day off for every day at work), of which 93 were given over to public games.

On an ordinary day, however, when there were no public games to amuse the people, the Romans stopped work in the early afternoon and then whiled away the time until the evening meal by taking a stroll, some more energetic form of physical exercise, or perhaps a bath. The rich might ride in a litter carried on the shoulders of their slaves, but most people simply promenaded along the bustling streets, using the carefully positioned stepping stones to cross from side to side and avoid the flowing sewage.

GAMES AND GAMBLING

Every now and then they would seek the peace of a public garden, the basilica steps in the Forum, or the shade of a portico, such as those in the Campus Martius, which, according to the philosopher Seneca, were places where even 'the most wretched could take his ease'. Here they spent an idle hour or two, gossiping or playing games.

The Roman enthusiasm for games and gambling was insatiable, despite a series of laws against it.

GAME OF CHANCE   The Romans enjoyed games of dice (left) in baths or taverns.

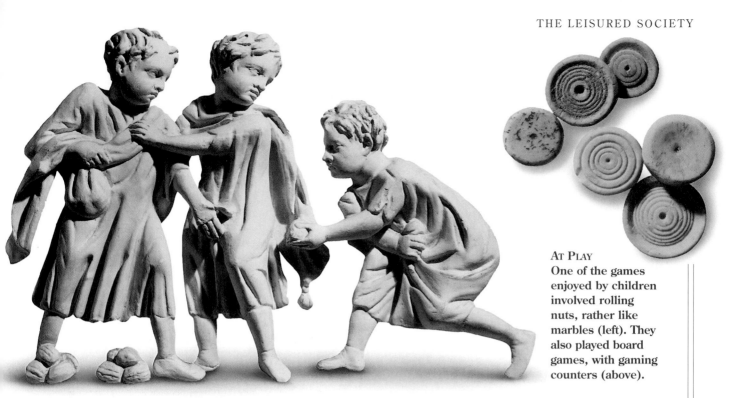

AT PLAY
One of the games enjoyed by children involved rolling nuts, rather like marbles (left). They also played board games, with gaming counters (above).

The writer Juvenal recorded 'men come not now with purses to the hazard of the gaming table, but with a treasure chest beside them . . . is it a simple form of madness to lose 100 000 sesterces and not have a shirt to give the shivering slave?' They gambled with bone dice, throwing a couple at a time from a container. The stakes were often quite high: according to the historian Suetonius, Emperor Nero risked '4000 gold pieces on each pip of the winning throw'. They also played *navia aut capita* (heads or tails) and *par impar*, in which players bet on whether their opponent held an odd or an even number of pebbles, knuckle-bones or nuts in his hand. The emperor Augustus himself was a fan of this particular game and is said to have issued friends and members of his family 250 denarii each to encourage them to bet. The game of *astragals* – sheep's foot bones – was also popular throughout the classical world. You threw four or five into the air and tried to catch them on the back of the hand or, if some fell to the ground, attempted to pick them off the floor without dropping any more.

Another game was *micatio*, a version of modern spoof. Each round, the players had simultaneously

---

EYEWITNESS

'HE WAS TAKING HIS EXERCISE IN SLIPPERS'

IN A STORY by Petronius, a group of friends meet at the baths to secure an invitation to dinner from the self-made millionaire, Trimalchio:
❛ We did not take our clothes off but began wandering around, or rather exchanging jokes while circulating among the little groups. Suddenly we saw a bald old man in a reddish shirt, playing ball with some long-haired boys. It was not so much the boys that made us watch . . . but the old gentleman himself. He was taking his exercise in slippers and throwing a green ball around. But he didn't pick it up if it touched the ground; instead there was a slave holding a bagful, and he supplied them to the players . . . Anyway, we entered the baths where we began sweating at once and we went immediately into the cold water. Trimalchio had been smothered in perfume and was already being rubbed down, not with linen towels, but with bathrobes of the finest wool. As this was going on, three masseurs sat drinking Falernian [high-quality wine] in front of him. Through quarrelling they spilled most of it and Trimalchio said they were drinking his health. . . .❜

BLOOD LUST **Cockfighting combined two interests of the Romans: bloodthirsty sport and gambling (note the bag of betting money on the table).**

to raise any number of fingers on their right hand, calling out their guess of the combined number of fingers raised. The winner was the first to call out the correct number of fingers raised by both players. Backgammon, chess and draughts (sometimes played on boards traced in the dust or scratched on the pavement) were also popular.

Taverns and inns were well patronised. Many had illegal gambling dens secreted in their back quarters; others hired prostitutes to serve as barmaids and were nothing more than bawdy houses. The largest brothel discovered in Pompeii consists of ten rooms, five on the ground floor and five above. Here, girls with exotic Greek and Oriental names would offer their services to clients for as little as two asses (small coins) – the price of two cups of wine.

The afternoon highlight for both sexes was the visit to the baths: indeed, for the orator Cicero, the gong that advertised the opening of the public baths each day was a sweeter sound

MATCH REFEREE **This detail from a mosaic, originally in the Baths of Caracalla in Rome, shows a judge of the games held there.**

than the voices of the philosophers in their schools. Even those who were wealthy enough to have a private bath at home visited the public baths as part of the day's social round. Men and women went at different times, since bathing was generally strictly segregated (mixed bathing had resulted in several scandals); however, men and women could visit the exercise courts at the same time.

ROMAN BATHS
The oldest baths in Pompeii, the Stabian Baths, date back to the 4th century BC and, as early as 33 BC, a census shows that there were 170 baths in Rome alone; by the 2nd century AD, the number was approaching 1000 (including 11 massive public baths). For adults, the cost of admission was minimal (about a quarter of an as), while children got in free. Just as politicians courted the people by providing shows and spectacles, they also built public baths or subsidised the entry fees: the military commander Agrippa, for instance, paid for everyone to visit the baths free for the course of his year as aedile in charge of public buildings.

A succession of Roman emperors – Titus, Trajan, Diocletian and Caracalla – all built public baths, which were supplied with water by the aqueducts. With their gymnasiums, shops, libraries and gardens, the baths were like luxury leisure centres. For example, the Baths of Diocletian, which were begun in AD 298, sprawled over 32 acres (13 ha) and could accommodate 3000 bathers. And at the second largest baths in the city, the Baths of Caracalla, 1500 bathers could enjoy art galleries, exercise courts or *palaestrae*, as well as the baths themselves.

SEA WORLD Magnificent mosaics in the Baths of Neptune at Ostia celebrate the world of the ancient sea god.

BATH TIME   A shaft of light pierces the gloom of the *calidarium*, or hot
room, of the Forum Baths in Pompeii, where customers worked up a
good sweat. The bathhouse mosaic (right) invites customers to 'have a
good bath' and asks them to take off their sandals on arrival.

'THE MAN WHO LIKES THE SOUND OF HIS VOICE IN THE BATH'

IN A LETTER to his friend Lucilius, the philosopher Seneca describes what it was like to live in an apartment above a public bath in Rome:

❦ Now imagine to yourself every kind of sound that can make one weary of one's years. When the strenuous types are doing their exercises, swinging weight-laden hands about, I hear the grumbling as they toil away – or go through the motions of toiling away – at them, and the hissings and strident gasps every time they expel their pent-up breath. When my attention turns to a less active fellow who is contenting himself with an ordinary inexpensive massage, I hear the smack of a hand pummelling his shoulders, the sound varying according as it comes down flat or cupped. But if on top of this some ball player comes along and starts shouting out the score, that's the end! Then add someone starting up a brawl, and someone else caught thieving, and the man who likes the sound of his voice in the bath, and the people who leap into the bath with a tremendous splash. Apart from those whose voices are, if nothing else, natural, think of the hair remover, continually giving vent to his shrill and penetrating cry in order to advertise his presence, never silent unless it be while he is plucking someone's armpits and making the client yell for him! Then think of the various cries of the man selling drinks, and the one selling sausages and the other selling pastries, and all the ones hawking for the catering shops, each publicising his wares with a distinctive cry of his own. ❦

Edward Gibbon, the 18th-century historian and author of *The Decline and Fall of the Roman Empire,* and the man who described history as 'little more than the register of the crimes, follies and misfortunes of mankind', could not contain his disapproval. Here, the author describes the public baths: '. . . The meanest Roman could purchase, with a small copper coin, the daily enjoyment of a scene of pomp and luxury which might excite the envy of the kings of Asia. From these stately palaces issued a swarm of dirty and ragged plebeians, without shoes and without a mantle, who loitered away whole days in the street or Forum to hear news and to hold disputes, who dissipated in extravagant gaming the miserable pittance of their wives and children, and spent the hours of the night in obscure taverns and brothels in the indulgence of gross and vulgar sensuality.'

On arrival, visitors might simply lounge around, sunbathing (a tan was thought healthy and virile), exchanging gossip, and playing board games, or they might work up a sweat, sprinting or exercising with dumbbells and balls filled with sand or air. Ball games such as trigon – a game of catch for three people – were particularly popular. And so was wrestling: the sportsmen stripped naked and covered themselves in oil and a fine sprinkling of dust to stop them becoming too slippery for their opponent's grip. Women, on the other hand, preferred the gentler pursuit of rolling hoops along with a stick.

Then it was time for the bath itself. Those who were still fully clothed undressed completely in the changing rooms before proceeding to the *tepidarium*, a large, vaulted hall that, as its name implies, was only gently heated. Next, they moved on to the *calidarium*, a hot room, rather like a Turkish bath, where the high temperature brought customers out in a healthy sweat. The bathers douched themselves with hot water from a large tub and had oil rubbed into their skin; the dirt and sweat was then scraped off by an assistant or a personal slave using a curved, razor-like implement known as a strigil. Then people cooled off gradually in the tepidarium before progressing to the large central hall, or *frigidarium*, and then to the *natatio*, or swimming pool, for an invigorating cold plunge.

CLEAN LIVING
A silver pail, found in the House of Menander in Pompeii, shows women helpers attending to the bath of the goddess Venus.

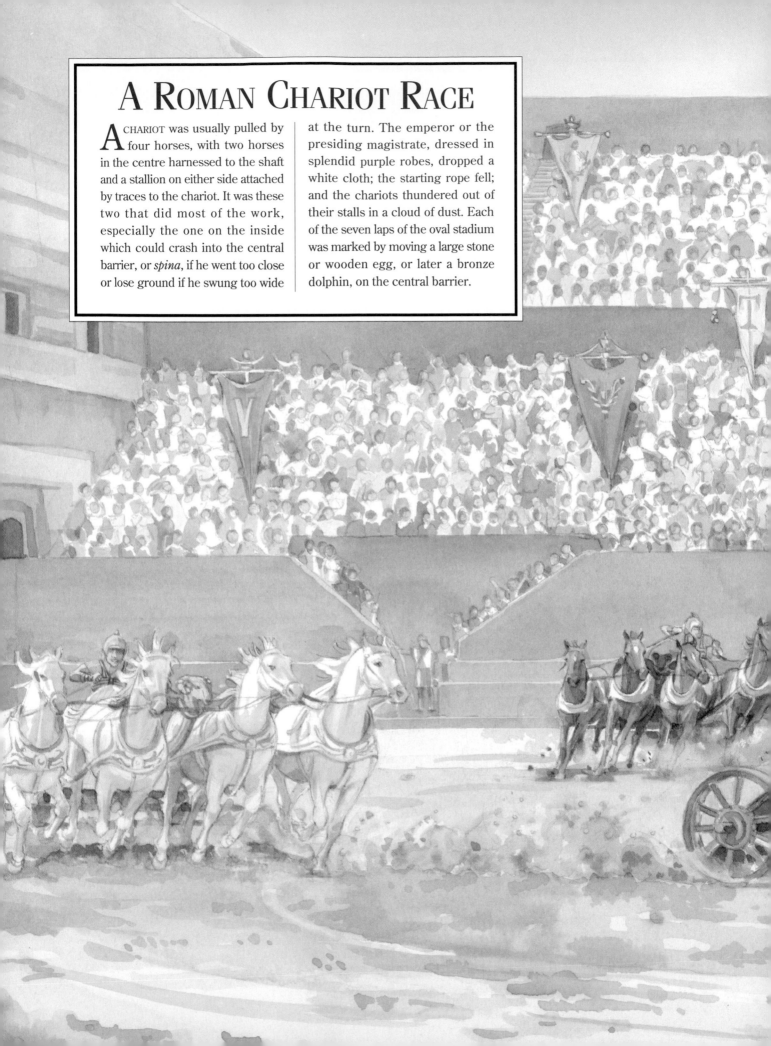

A ROMAN CHARIOT RACE

A CHARIOT was usually pulled by four horses, with two horses in the centre harnessed to the shaft and a stallion on either side attached by traces to the chariot. It was these two that did most of the work, especially the one on the inside which could crash into the central barrier, or *spina*, if he went too close or lose ground if he swung too wide at the turn. The emperor or the presiding magistrate, dressed in splendid purple robes, dropped a white cloth; the starting rope fell; and the chariots thundered out of their stalls in a cloud of dust. Each of the seven laps of the oval stadium was marked by moving a large stone or wooden egg, or later a bronze dolphin, on the central barrier.

SHOWS AND SPECTACLES

'Nothing is more damaging than wasting time at the games,'

the philosopher Seneca complained. 'It is then that vice steals

secretly upon you through the avenue of pleasure.'

AS IN SO MANY aspects of their cultural life, Roman theatre was influenced by the Greeks. The first play to be staged in Rome, in 240 BC, was a translation by a former slave called Livius Andronicus of a Greek drama, and was performed as part of a religious festival. For several hundred years, the popularity of plays – particularly comedies by Plautus and Terence – can be judged by the size of the theatres themselves. The Theatre of Pompey, Rome's first permanent stone theatre, dedicated in 55 BC, could seat around 27 000 people. Previous theatres had been makeshift wooden structures, usually set into the sides of a hill. And the Theatre of Marcellus, which was commissioned by Emperor Augustus to commemorate his son-in-law who had died at the age of 20, could hold up to 20 000 people. These were massive buildings, compared with the world's largest purpose-built theatre today, the Perth Entertainment Centre in Western Australia with 8500 seats.

Given their size, it is hardly surprising that there was nothing intimate or subtle about the types of play performed there: indeed, it was quite hard to hear what was going on and the actors had to wear masks so that they were easily identifiable. Most plays were spectacles: fabulous triumphs of set design and special effects, with gods descending from the heights to the roar of imitation thunder; musicals with dancing and songs which the audience joined in; tragedies with bloodcurdling tales of murder and mayhem; and mimes, which resembled bedroom farces and featured unmasked actors and sometimes naked actresses. The audience was quick to signal its appreciation or otherwise – snapping their fingers and thumbs to show approval, clapping or waving their togas for enthusiasm, and whistling or hissing when dissatisfied.

BACKGROUND MUSIC Players of musical instruments accompanied the gladiatorial combats.

Despite these attractions, the classical theatre rapidly lost its audience to games in the amphitheatre in which gladiators duelled to the death. And the plays themselves came more and more to resemble the spectacles staged in the arena. One play, for instance, performed during the reign of Emperor Domitian, ended with a scene in which a condemned criminal took the place of the actor and was tortured to death on stage. Some plays were even performed in the amphitheatre itself, with criminals performing mythological scenes, such as Orpheus being devoured by wild animals – but, in this case, the action was real.

Horse-racing was very popular with the Romans. As with many other aspects of Roman life, its rituals

PLAY ACTING
In this mosaic, actors don the masks that make their roles clear even from a distance.

UNDERNEATH THE ARCHES From the street, visitors entered the Colosseum through a series of circular inside corridors, from which sloping aisles, or *vomitoria,* led off into the amphitheatre itself.

recalled the early days of the city. For example, after the races held each year on October 15 in the Forum, the winning horse was sacrificed by the priests of the temple of Mars to commemorate the religious rite practised by the early Romans on their annual return from war. Its blood was collected in two large bowls, one of which was poured over the hearth of the home of the *Pontifex Maximus* (the chief priest), while the other was sent to the Vestal Virgins for use in their religious ceremonies. The horse's head was decorated with bread loaves and fought over by the people living along the Via Sacra and the inhabitants of the area known as the Suburra, both of whom were determined to have the honour of displaying this gruesome trophy on their walls.

A Day at the Races

The races held at the three Roman circuses – the Circus Flaminius, the Circus of Gaius and, largest of all, the Circus Maximus – drew crowds from all over the city. According to Pliny the Elder, the Circus Maximus had 255 000 seats – making it larger than the Strahov Stadium in Prague, the world's biggest open-air stadium today. The spectators might include the emperor and his family in the imperial box which jutted out from the Palatine Hill; on a good day, if the emperor was feeling particularly generous, he might distribute raffle tickets to the crowd – with cash, or even a ship or a farm, as the prize.

There were various types of race – in one, the *desultores,* or jockeys, guided two horses at once, leaping from the back of one to the back of the other. The main business of the day, however, was chariot racing. There were up to 24 races a day in the time of Caligula, each consisting of four four-horse

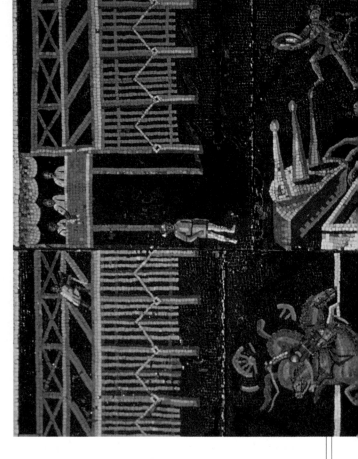

STARTER'S ORDERS
A consul starts a chariot race by throwing his handkerchief on to the track.

chariots, or *quadrigae*, although there might be up to 12 smaller chariots in a single race. Each quadriga represented what the Romans called a *factio* or team. There were four of these, usually allied in pairs: the Whites and the Greens, the Blues and the Reds. Each of the teams maintained great establishments of riders, vets, stablehands, saddlers and, of course, the horses themselves – raised in the far-flung stud farms of the Roman Empire and followed by the ancient Romans for their form and pedigree as closely as racehorses are today. The aptly named Victor, for example, had 429 wins to his name.

Betting and bribery were rife and, in the highly competitive world of the factions, a successful charioteer could earn a fortune. A charioteer named Diocles retired in AD 150 with a fortune of 35 million sesterces, having competed 4257 times and won 1462 times.

Several Roman emperors, including Augustus and Domitian, attempted to introduce Greek-style

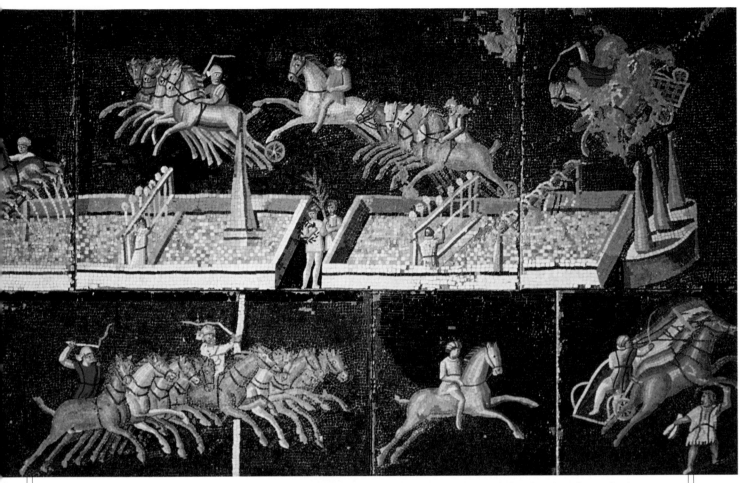

CHARIOT RACE In the centre of the track, race officials hold up the palm and wreath for the victorious charioteer.

games to Rome, with programmes that included both athletics and the arts. But competitions for sprinting and discus-throwing, poetry and music never really caught on, for the Romans preferred their spectacles to be far more blood-thirsty. From the 2nd century BC, they enjoyed games in which gladiators fought each other to the death.

Like the horse-races, the gladiatorial games had their origins in the rites of ancient Rome. At first, they were no more than small private functions when the family gathered at the ancestral tomb on the outskirts of the city to mourn the death

TEAM COLOURS A jockey wears the distinctive colours of one of the four teams – the Reds.

of a relative. Believing that the spilling of human blood somehow appeased the soul of the dead ancestor, they deputed a couple of slaves to fight to the death. It was not long, however, before the politicians had hijacked this ancient custom and, in a bid to enhance their own reputations, were organising increasingly elaborate funerals – with games – whenever the occasion arose and staging them in the Forum. Even if there was no obvious occasion, they would invent one: a triumph, for example, for a great general; or a memorial service for a famous

continued on page 106

THE ROMANS AT PLAY

THE FESTIVAL YEAR

Official calendars gave the Romans a regular timetable

for feasts in honour of the gods.

JANUARY: COMPITALIA
Farmers erected a shrine on the borders of their farm, and a sacrifice was made to herald a prosperous new year. In the towns, hens were sacrificed at each crossroads – and the whole neighbourhood joined in the festivities.

FEBRUARY 13-21: PARENTALIA
The Romans paid their respects to their dead parents, placing food on their graves to prevent them feeling hungry; the festival ended with a family dinner.

FEBRUARY 15: LUPERCALIA
Two teams of young men assembled at the Lupercal, a cave on the Palatine, and sprinted around the hill, dressed in goatskins and smeared with blood. In a ritual that was believed to encourage fertility, they lashed out with long strips of goatskin at the barren women who had lined up along the way.

ANIMAL SACRIFICE   A bull is prepared for sacrifice – a central feature of many Roman festivals.

MARCH 1: MATRONALIA
The perpetual fire was re-kindled in the Temple of Vesta in Rome by rubbing two sticks together.

MARCH 14
Romans celebrated the feast of Mars, god of war, with horse-races in the Campus Martius.

MARCH 15
On the Ides of March, people crossed the River Tiber and picnicked on the far bank. It was said that you would continue to live for as many years as the cups of wine you drank.

MARCH 23: TUBILISTRIUM
The battle trumpets were purified – in a bid for success during the forthcoming season of war.

APRIL 4–10: LUDI MEGALENSES
Games were held in honour of Cybele, the Great Mother.

APRIL 12-19: LUDI CERIALES
Games were held in honour of Ceres, goddess of corn.

APRIL 21: PARILIA
At the feast of Pales, the goddess of herds, the Romans celebrated the birthday of their city with bonfires and feasting.

APRIL 28-MAY 3: LUDI FLORALES
Festival games were held in the Circus Maximus in honour of the goddess Flora.

JUNE 9: VESTALIA
Wives took food to the Temple of Vesta.

JUNE 24: FORS FORTUNA
The Romans rowed down the Tiber to the shrines honouring the goddess Fortuna.

THE IDES OF JULY
Young cavalrymen paraded to the Forum, where sacrifices were made at the Temple of Castor and Pollux.

JULY 20–30: LUDI VICTORIAE CAESARIS
Games commemorated Julius Caesar's victories in Gaul.

JULY 6-13: LUDI APOLLINARES
The god Apollo was celebrated with shows and spectacles.

AUGUST 12
The sacrifice of a heifer to the Greek Hercules initiated a public feast, which was funded by traders and shopkeepers who contributed 10 per cent of their profits at the shrine of the god.

SONG AND DANCE   Naked revellers, in this wall-painting from the 1st century AD, celebrate Bacchus, the god of wine.

AUGUST 13
A feast to Diana, goddess of hunting.

AUGUST 21
The Feast of Consus, the god of the granary.

AUGUST 27: VOLTURNIA
Feasts were held to protect the ripening grapes.

SEPTEMBER 5-19: LUDI ROMANI
The Roman Games consisted of theatre, games and races. One of the earliest games devoted to the gods as a gesture of appeasement at times of crisis, the first Roman Games were held in 366 BC.

OCTOBER 15
A horse-race in the Forum took place on the Ides of the month. After the race, the right-hand horse of the winning chariot was sacrificed to Mars, the god of war.

NOVEMBER 4-17: LUDI PLEBEII
Shows and spectacles for the masses.

DECEMBER 17: SATURNALIA
This festival consisted of six days of celebration, when the world was turned upside down. Schools were closed and masters waited on their slaves at table. Rather like a pagan Christmas, people exchanged presents, such as candles and – for children – clay dolls purchased at one of the seasonal fairs.

AT THE ALTAR   In a frieze, dating from the 1st century AD, sacrificial animals are led to the altar, where they will be slaughtered by temple officials.

RACE DAY
On this tomb of
a circus
magistrate (left),
chariots – each
ridden by a
single driver –
career around
seven laps of
the racetrack.

person, or simply a member of their extended family. As the politicians attempted to outdo each other, these games developed into displays of unrelieved cruelty.

Election candidates courted the public by funding such spectacles, despite the laws passed to prevent vote-buying of this sort. But Caesar and the emperors who followed him were acutely conscious of the propaganda value of the games and took every opportunity to stage the most impressive spectacles in order to command the loyalty of the mob – even though the people no longer had any votes to be bought. Augustus, for example, limited the amount of money that others could spend on public games but gave three *munera*, or gifts as the games were called, in his own honour and five in honour of his sons and grandsons. He was to claim in his autobiography that he had shown some 10 000 gladiators during his 40-year reign. And Trajan, according to the 3rd-century historian Dio Cassius, 'always looked with great attention to the stars of the theatre, circus and arena; for he well knew that the

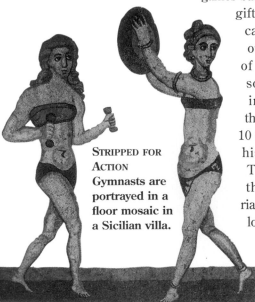

STRIPPED FOR
ACTION
Gymnasts are
portrayed in a
floor mosaic in
a Sicilian villa.

measure of excellence in government lies no less in the amusements it provides than in its care for more important matters, and that although the distribution of grain and money allowances satisfies each citizen taken individually, the spectacle is necessary to make content the people as a whole'.

As the emperors gave better and better games, so the public craved more and more – in a vicious circle of ever-growing and more inventive cruelty. No single building symbolised more the way in which gladiatorial games lay at the foundations of imperial power than the Colosseum. After the great fire of AD 64 had destroyed the city's first permanent amphitheatre (a circular stadium, as opposed to the traditional semicircular theatre), successive emperors authorised the building of a massive, four-storeyed amphitheatre, known since the Middle Ages as the Colosseum, where 45 000 at a time could enjoy the spectacle of the gladiatorial games, wild animal fights and animal hunts.

PREPARING FOR A DAY AT THE GAMES
In the provinces, gladiators were provided for public games – at a price – by contractors engaged by the municipal authorities. The contractor, or *lanista*, recruited his gladiators from the poor, from slaves whom he had bought specially for the purpose, and from young men in search of fame and fortune who vowed to be 'burnt with fire, shackled with chains, whipped with rods and killed with steel' for the duration of their contract. He trained them and housed them in barracks. In Rome, however,

A Monument to Murder

THE COLOSSEUM was the ultimate expression of imperial power and grandeur. It took nine years to build, contained more than 100 000 blocks of stone each weighing four tons, and 300 tons of metal to support the structure. You entered the building from the street through one of 80 arches into a series of circular inside corridors and stairways which led to the sloping aisles, or *vomitoria*; these disgorged members of the crowd into the appropriate stand, enabling them to be seated within ten minutes of arrival.

The seating arrangements were a microcosm of Roman society. The emperor and his consuls, courtiers and the Vestal Virgins sat in a box right on the edge of the arena, with the lower social classes and women occupying seats progressively farther away – the top terrace was reserved for the lowest classes. To protect the crowd from the midday sun, there was an awning, supported on poles attached to the top storey and arching over the entire arena; this was anchored by rope to bollards outside the building.

The arena itself was made of wood and covered with sand imported from Egypt; it was surrounded by a wall, with a fence on top to prevent the performers from escaping. Underneath the arena was a network of tunnels stretching for a mile. It was here that the animals were kept in subterranean cages, which were winched to a higher level by pulleys; the animals were then herded with firebrands along wooden walkways, up a ramp and into the arena. On occasions, the arena of

MAN AND BEAST   A spear-carrying gladiator does battle with a lion.

the Colosseum was flooded to provide the setting for a *naumachia*, or mock sea battle.

INTO THE ARENA   The terraces of the Colosseum rise above the unpaved arena; below lies a network of corridors and service rooms.

'THIS FUTILE, TEDIOUS, MONOTONOUS BUSINESS'

IN A LETTER to Calvisius Rufus, a town councillor of Como, Pliny the Younger congratulates himself on his use of the spare time:

❛ I have been spending all the last few days among my notes and papers in most welcome peace. How could I – in the city? The Races were on, a type of spectacle which has never had the slightest attraction for me. I can find nothing new or different in them: once seen is enough, so it surprises me all the more that so many thousands of adult men should have such a childish passion for watching galloping horses and drivers standing in chariots, over and over again. If they were attracted by the speed of the horses or the drivers' skill one could account for it, but in fact it is the racing colours they really support and care about, and if the colours were to be exchanged in mid-course during a race, they would transfer their favour and enthusiasm and rapidly desert the famous drivers and horses whose names they shout as they recognise them from afar. Such is the popularity and importance of a worthless shirt – I don't mean with the crowd, which is worth less than the shirt, but with certain serious individuals. When I think how this futile, tedious, monotonous business can keep them sitting endlessly in their seats, I take pleasure in the fact that their pleasure is not mine. And I have been very glad to fill my idle hours with literary work during these days which others have wasted. . . . ❜

gladiators were recruited from prisoners of war and criminals who had been condemned to death, and trained in special schools. The night before the fight, they were treated to a sumptuous last supper, which ghoulish members of the public were invited to witness.

EXERCISE CLASS   Under the watchful eye of their master, gladiators exercise with dumbbells.

Preparations for the games began first thing in the morning. As the crowds began to arrive – many having camped out on the streets or rooftops of the city – the animals were brought in from holding pens outside the city. Bewildered and terrified, they were herded into the cages beneath the arena by trained handlers. After a parade around the arena by gladiators shouting 'We who are about to die salute you!' to the emperor, the animals were released into the arena at about 9 am for the first event of the day: the wild-beast hunt.

One emperor, Galba, tried to tempt the public with such novelties as tightrope-walking elephants. But the Romans were really far more fascinated by the notion of nature red in tooth and claw, and the show's organisers did their best to create realistic sets for this event, constructing little hills, trees and even lakes in the arena. To the accompaniment of music from a band of horn players and a hydraulic organ, the animals were hunted through this landscape, and their carcasses swiftly removed by attendants through the 'gate of death' at one end. The range of exotic animals on display was a symbol of Rome's conquest of the Mediterranean basin, and especially their penetration into Africa: hippopotamuses, giraffes, bears, panthers, bulls, lions, leopards, crocodiles and tigers. In a letter, Pliny congratulates Valerius Maximus for putting on a show in Verona as a funeral tribute to his late wife, and is only 'sorry the African panthers you had bought in such quantities did not turn up on the appointed day, but you deserve the credit although the weather prevented their arriving in time; it was not your fault that you could not show them'.

The slaughter was horrific: 5000 beasts on a single day of the games lasting 100 days with which the Colosseum was opened in AD 80. Eventually, the empire's wild animal resources were depleted – the lion becoming extinct in the Middle East and the elephant in North Africa – and beasts had to be imported from farther and farther afield.

Around the middle of the morning, there was another animal show. This time, criminals who had been condemned *ad bestias* ('to the beasts') – rather than to crucifixion or burning – were thrown to the animals, as the band continued with relentless gaiety. In case the lions were frightened or reluctant, the criminals might be tethered to stakes from which they

ANIMAL KILL In a mosaic from North Africa, two gladiators slay a leopard.

could not escape, and a lump of raw meat hung from them as extra bait. There might also be a fight in which animals were pitted against each other – a rhinoceros against a lion, say.

By noon the whole arena stank in the sweltering midday sun. Despite the best efforts of the attendants to rake new sand over the bloodstained arena, the reek of animal and human carnage was appalling – relieved only partially by the burning of incense and the sprinkling of the crowd with perfume from

A DAY IN THE LIFE OF
A GLADIATOR OF THE IMPERIAL SCHOOL

THE SUN HAD not yet risen over Rome's massive amphitheatre, but the inmates of a nearby building were already being roused from sleep, and herded from their cells, by guards. Felix was one of almost 2000 men at Emperor Hadrian's Ludus Magnus, a gladiator school. He had been sent there for trying to escape from his slave-master; his comrades included criminals, prisoners of war, and citizens who had fallen on hard times.

As they trooped into breakfast, Felix remembered how all of them – including those lunatics who had enrolled for the sheer hell of it – had been forced to swear the same oath: accepting, as punishment, 'to be burnt, to be chained up, to be beaten, and to be killed by an iron weapon'. Like most of the other meals, breakfast consisted of a large bowl of barley porridge – food fit only for animals, thought Felix. But he also noticed how much weight he had put on at the school, which at least gave him some padding against sword-cuts. In the central courtyard, the gladiators

assembled for weightlifting and lessons in swordsmanship. As he parried and thrust at a stake in the ground with a practice wooden sword and wicker buckler, Felix realised how much his chances of survival in the arena depended on this training. If he survived for three years, he might never have to fight again. A further two years, and he might be a free man. It was this thought, rather than the prize money for a successful fight, or the cheers of the crowd that sustained him for the rest of the day.

FIGHT TO THE DEATH In a terracotta relief, gladiators with swords, shields, helmets and leg-protectors do battle in the amphitheatre.

special fountains. But the show was not yet even halfway through. It was now time for the mass executions, when hundreds of criminals were simply driven into the arena and attacked by armed men, their screams drowning the band.

At around 2 pm, the gladiators were handed their weapons: a net and a trident for the *retiarius;* a helmet and a sword for the *murmillo*; a stabbing sword for the *secutor*; a short sword, shield and helmet for the Samnite prisoner of war; and a curved scimitar and small shield for the Thracian; and so on. Next, each gladiator was pitted against his opponent, either of the same category (blind people were sometimes armed and pitted against each other) or, exhibiting a particularly Roman taste for the grotesque, against a completely different type of warrior: a murmillo against a retiarius, or a woman against a dwarf. And the band played on. The butchery was on a massive scale: in one set of games, which took place over a five-year period in the 2nd century AD, 4941 pairs of gladiators participated.

Most fights were to the death, which officials would make sure of by hitting the fallen fighter on the head with a mallet; the dead man would then be stretchered off

the blood-soaked sand by an attendant dressed, perhaps, as Charon, the mythical ferryman of the underworld. But there was an alternative. The loser could appeal to the crowd for mercy by raising his left arm. If the spectators raised their thumbs in response and shouted *mitte* ('let him go'), the emperor, who presided over the games, generally lifted his thumb and the loser would be carried out of the arena. If the crowd turned their thumbs down, crying *iugula* ('slay him'), the emperor inverted his thumb to pass the death sentence. It was a rare opportunity for the crowd, who had lost their votes under the emperors, to exercise their collective will. A gladiator who had won a great many times not only achieved pop-star status with the public, but he might also be awarded a wooden sword at the end of the fight, signifying his freedom.

It was not until the 4th and 5th centuries that the butcheries were gradually brought to an end. The games and the constant search for novelty had been ruinously expensive. As the empire collapsed, massive supplies of animal and human fodder became less available – and eventually, in AD 549, the last games were held in Rome.

HEAD CASE The bronze helmet of a Thracian gladiator completely covered his head and face.

MIND, BODY AND SPIRIT

The tomb of the Haterii, a wealthy family of builders, looks rather like
an extremely elaborate temple. In this relief, mourners attend the
laying out of the body of the deceased. Performing the last rites
of an ancient Roman was an occasion of great ceremony,
celebrating a life that, despite considerable sophistication
in certain branches of medicine, averaged only 30 years.

HEALTH AND HEALING

The ancient Romans performed some quite sophisticated surgical operations.

But most of their everyday medical practices were based

on a combination of blind faith and folklore.

MEDICINE for the Romans was a mixture of superstition and science. On the one hand, people trusted in folk remedies that had been handed down from generation to generation. The politician and writer Cato the Elder (234-149 BC), for example, treated his household with remedies from a book that had been in his family for several generations: juniper-wood wine for sciatica, pomegranate extract for colic and worms, and cabbage for pretty much everything, from aches and pains to insomnia and deafness. On the other hand, wealthier people often patronised professional doctors who had been trained in Greece. However, these doctors' Greek training meant that they were viewed with suspicion by the more traditional Romans. According to Cato, 'the Greeks . . . are a quite worthless people, and an intractable one . . . When that race gives us its literature it will corrupt all things, and even the more if it sends hither its physicians. They have conspired together to murder all foreigners with their physic.'

The Roman belief that everything that happened was in the hands of the gods inclined them to a certain fatalism; there was little room, as there is today, for concepts such as prevention, diagnosis and prognosis. If you fell ill, there was little you could do about it, except pray to the gods and treat the specific symptoms

(rather than their cause) with folk remedies. Even when physicians started to apply more scientific methods, most people – including the doctors themselves – continued to believe, first and foremost, in the powers of the healing deities.

FAITH HEALING

For the ancient Greeks and Romans alike, the most respected of these gods was Aesculapius (Asklepios in Greek), who was generally portrayed carrying a staff festooned with serpents. The cult of Asklepios had been popular in Greece since the 5th century BC – notably at Epidauros – but a healing centre was also established at Rome, on the island in the middle of the Tiber, in 292 BC. This was still flourishing in the 2nd century AD, when reports of miracle cures performed there included that of a certain Julian, who 'was spitting up blood and had been despaired of by all men' when 'the god revealed that he should go and from the three-fold altar take the seeds of a pine cone and eat them with honey for three days. And he was saved. . .'.

Healing shrines, dedicated to Aesculapius like the one at Rome

HEALING DEITIES
The ancient god Aesculapius (left), leans on his staff with Telesphorus, the god of convalescence, at his feet. Right: Hygieia, goddess of health.

HEALING WATERS   The Roman baths at Aquae Sulis (Bath), rebuilt in the 18th century, were fed by hot springs.

or to Apollo, spread throughout the empire. Many of them were sited beside mineral springs, where people took the waters to cure their complaints – a practice that continued until recently in cases of gout, rheumatism and arthritis. For example, at Bath (Aquae Sulis) in England, a stone carving depicting Aesculapius has been found in one of the thermal springs; and at Aachen (Aquae Granni), Apollo shared responsibility for the springs with a local Germanic god, Grannus. As in many Roman

BODY PARTS   Terracotta votives – here, an ear and an eye – were offered to the gods in the hope of a cure.

Catholic Churches in Italy today, it was quite common at healing shrines for people to make offerings of a leg, a foot, an eye, a head or a breast (usually in terracotta) to indicate the part of the anatomy that was afflicted.

A MORE SCIENTIFIC APPROACH

From the 2nd century BC onwards, Greek doctors started to settle in Rome in large numbers; and gradually the Roman authorities began to recognise their professional status. In 46 BC, Julius Caesar granted them their citizenship, and just over 20 years later, the emperor Augustus rewarded them with immunity from tax. Some of them were even retained by the municipal authorities in provincial towns to provide a public health service.

One of the problems, however, was that there was no formal training and no formal qualification.

After an apprenticeship with a practising doctor – or, if you were rich, after attending a medical centre in, say, Athens, Alexandria or Ephesus – you simply set yourself up as a doctor, making house calls or practising from a rented booth or a few rooms in your own home.

It is hardly surprising, then, that so many writers considered the 'profession' to be full of charlatans and quacks. 'Until recently, Diaulus was a doctor,' joked Martial in one of his epigrams, 'now he is an undertaker. He is still doing, as an undertaker, what he used to do as a doctor.' Even the level-headed Pliny the Younger complained that 'there is no doubt that all these physicians, in their hunt for popularity by means of some novelty, do not hesitate to buy it with our lives . . . Hence too that gloomy inscription on monuments: "It was the crowd of physicians that killed me." '

The medical teaching introduced by these Greek-trained doctors was very different from the ancient combination of faith and folklore. For a start, they believed in preventive medicine, and stressed the importance of moderation in eating and drinking, of exercise, and of a healthy balance between work and play. They also practised the more modern techniques of diagnosis and prognosis – identifying an illness and then predicting its likely course from previous experience of similar complaints.

Most of their treatments were based on the theory of the four humours, which claimed that illnesses were caused by an imbalance of yellow bile, black

---

EYEWITNESS

'USE THE ASHES OF A DEER'S ANTLERS'

IN HIS 37 VOLUME *Natural History*, the Roman administrator and encyclopedic writer Pliny the Elder (AD 23-79) describes a few remedies of doubtful efficacy:

❦ A cure for jaundice: use the ashes of a deer's antlers, the blood of an ass diluted with wine, or the first manure excreted by an ass foal after its birth, in a quantity the size of a bean, mixed with wine. The potion cures the disease within three days.

A quick remedy for broken bones: the ashes of the jawbone of a boar or pig. Or lard boiled and then packed around the broken bone mends it with amazing rapidity. For fractures of the ribs, goat's manure mixed in wine is particularly recommended.

Strains and injuries received from a blow are treated with wild boar's manure which has been collected in the springtime and dried. This same treatment works for chariot drivers who have been dragged or run over or badly bruised in any way, even if the manure is smeared on while still fresh. ❦

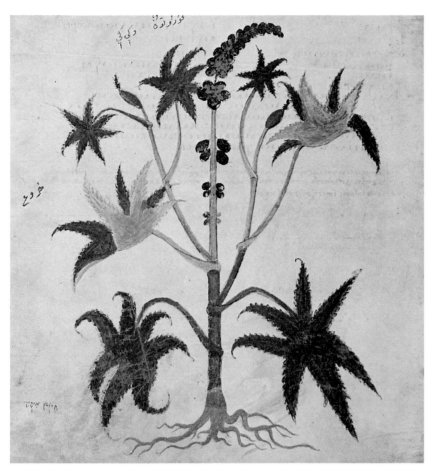

HERBAL REMEDY The castor-oil plant was one of many medicinal plants described by the 1st-century pharmacologist, Dioscorides.

some 600 different herbal remedies – the ingredients for many of which would have been available locally. Others could only have been acquired from specialist dealers: for example, balsam essence and resin, which were used in poultices and eye salves, came from Syria; and *lycium,* which was used to staunch bleeding, came from Asia Minor and farther east.

COMMON COMPLAINTS AND CURES

Many illnesses were believed, particularly by moralists, to be the preserve of the rich – the direct result of their celebrated overindulgence. According to the philosopher Seneca, these complaints included 'paleness, and a trembling of wine-sodden muscles, and a repulsive thinness, due rather to indigestion than to hunger. Thence weak, tottering steps, and a reeling gait just like that of drunkenness. Thence dropsy, spreading under the entire skin, and the belly growing to a paunch through an ill habit of taking more than it can hold. Thence yellow jaundice, discoloured countenances, and bodies that rot inwardly, and fingers that grow knotty when the joints stiffen, and muscles that are numbed and without power of feeling, and palpitation of the heart with its ceaseless pounding . . . Why should I mention the other innumerable diseases, the tortures that result from high living?'

Rich and poor alike, however, would have suffered

bile, blood or phlegm in the body. To remove an excess of one of these (or, indeed, some other harmful substance), doctors might prescribe sweating it out in the hot-room at the public baths. More radical techniques included purging the body with an enema or with a laxative concoction of aloes or hellebore; and bloodletting. The physician made an incision in the vein, usually in the arm, and attached a 'bleeding cup' of glass, bronze or horn – with openings at both ends – to the cut. The opening at one end of the cup nestled around the wound, while the physician sucked at the other end (or placed some burning lint through the opening) to create a vacuum which secured the cup to the arm. Blood, drawn by the vacuum, then flowed from the vein into the cup.

Doctors also prescribed a whole range of herbal medicines and ointments, some of which might have done some good and many of which would only have worked as placebos. Centaury, for example, was used to treat snakebites; fenugreek for pleurisy and pneumonia; and plantain for dysentery. In his writings, the physician Galen described

MEDICINE WOMAN
In this relief,
a pharmacist (a woman,
unusually) sits in her
shop, surrounded by
the tools of the trade.

DOCTOR TO THE EMPEROR

AS THE MEMBER of a wealthy family from Pergamum in Asia Minor, Galen (AD 129-99) could afford to study at some of the best medical centres in the ancient world: first at Pergamum itself and then in Smyrna, Corinth and Alexandria. In AD 162, however, he moved to Rome where his experience and his brilliance as an anatomist (learned partly as the surgeon to a school of gladiators) became well known.

Several spectacular cures of influential people swiftly propelled him into the upper reaches of Roman society, where he treated the emperor Marcus Aurelius.

Galen's greatest legacy, however, consists of the 21 surviving volumes of medical and philosophical writings that were to influence the practice of medicine in Europe until at least the 17th century. These writings were, in part, reassessments and refinements of existing – and predominantly Greek – medical knowledge. But some of his teachings broke new ground: for example, his understanding that blood nourishes the tissues of the body, and that the brain controls our powers of speech; and his knowledge – demonstrated during animal vivisections – of the way in which digestion works. Where, perhaps, his legacy was less helpful was in his attachment to the theory of humours, which suggested that imbalances of blood, bile and phlegm could be corrected by diet, drugs, sweating and bloodletting.

from common complaints such as food poisoning, diarrhoea and dysentery; and from intestinal parasites, such as worms, which were probably caused by eating contaminated meat and then spread by poor sanitation and communal lavatories. Many people also suffered from skin complaints, such as psoriasis, and eye diseases, such as trachoma, ophthalmia and corneal scars, which doctors treated with eye salves and ointment sticks.

There was a whole range of illnesses, caused by malnutrition and vitamin deficiencies, to which the poor were particularly vulnerable: scurvy from a diet low in fresh fruit and vegetables, and rickets caused by a lack of vitamin D found in dairy products and fish-liver oil. Their teeth were worn down by a constant diet of gritty bread and gruel; and

years of backbreaking work precipitated the early onset of osteoarthritis. In the overcrowded conditions of the city, acute infectious diseases such as polio, tetanus, typhus, pneumonia and meningitis spread with great speed, while chronic diseases such as leprosy and pulmonary tuberculosis lingered

GOING TO THE DOCTOR
Medical instruments hanging from the roof, and the snake (symbol of Aesculapius) entwined around the tree, mark the profession of this physician in a funerary relief.

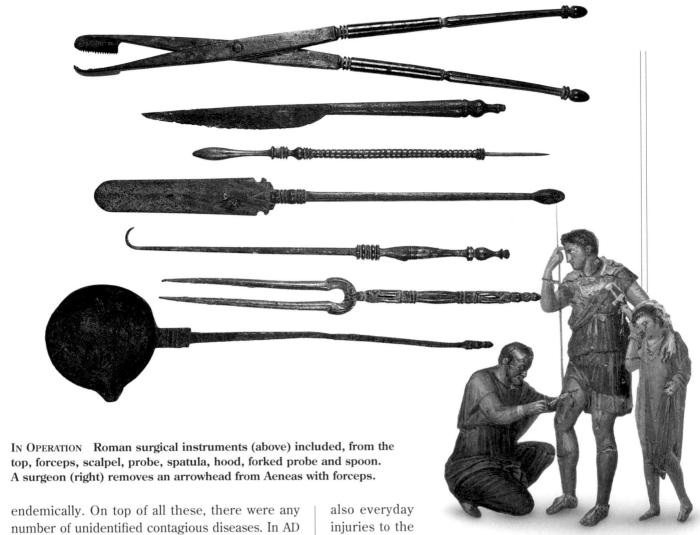

IN OPERATION Roman surgical instruments (above) included, from the top, forceps, scalpel, probe, spatula, hood, forked probe and spoon. A surgeon (right) removes an arrowhead from Aeneas with forceps.

endemically. On top of all these, there were any number of unidentified contagious diseases. In AD 65, for example, some 30 000 were reported to have died of an epidemic in Rome. Further plagues continued to devastate the city – particularly in AD 165 (when Marcus Aurelius tried and failed to stop the spread of disease with a series of religious ceremonies), in AD 180 and in AD 251-66, when 5000 were said to be dying a day in Rome alone.

In addition to the dangers of disease, there were also everyday injuries to the body, which were treated with wine, vinegar, pitch and turpentine, and then bandaged. Many of these wounds must have turned gangrenous and eventually necessitated amputation of the affected limb and the attachment of a wooden prosthesis. Apart from painkilling draughts, made perhaps from the boiled root of white mandrake, henbane and the juice from wild poppies (which included opium), these operations were performed without anaesthetic and must have been bloody ordeals of stark terror and excruciating pain. It can have been of little comfort to the patient that the bronze or iron instruments used by the surgeon – scalpels, fine-toothed saws, probes and forceps – were of the highest quality and precision.

Some physicians were extremely accomplished. In the 1st century AD, Cornelius Celsus described tooth removal, the setting of broken bones and complex surgical operations.

DRUG PRESCRIPTION

It has been estimated that up to 40 per cent of the drugs recommended by the 1st-century pharmacologist Dioscorides would actually have helped his patients. Many of them are similar in their chemical composition to drugs prescribed today. Thymum (as in thymol), for example, was antiseptic and not dissimilar to the carbolic acid used by Joseph Lister 18 centuries later.

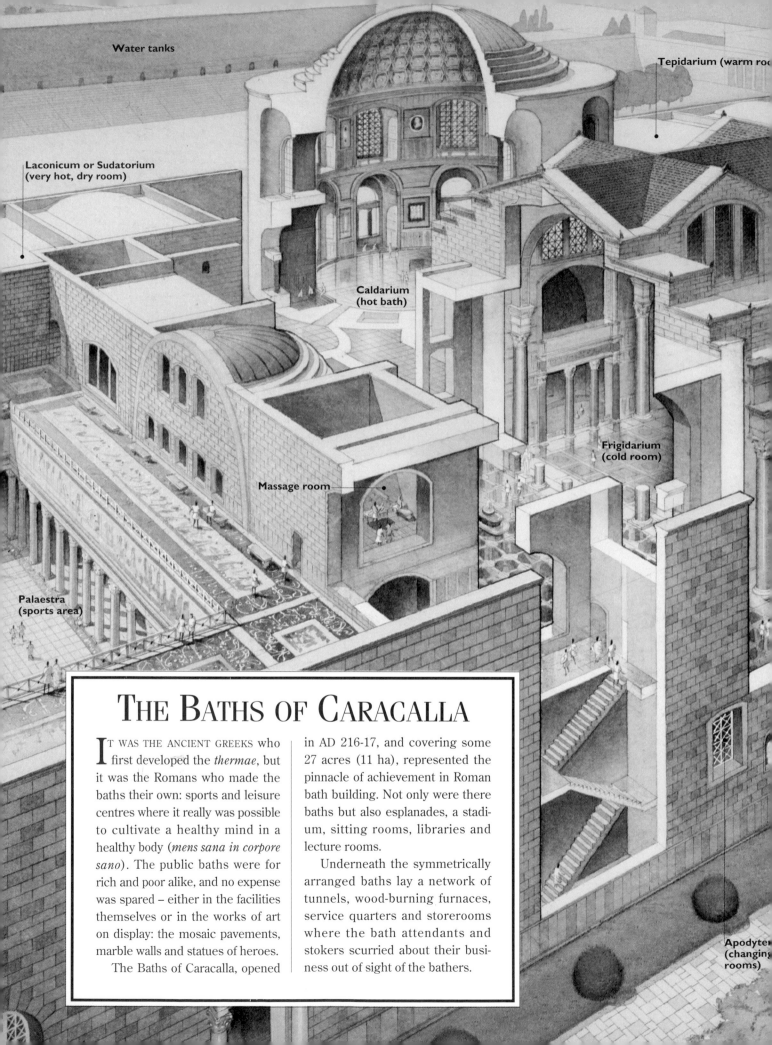

Water tanks

Tepidarium (warm roo[m])

Laconicum or Sudatorium
(very hot, dry room)

Caldarium
(hot bath)

Frigidarium
(cold room)

Massage room

Palaestra
(sports area)

Apodyter[ium]
(changing
rooms)

THE BATHS OF CARACALLA

IT WAS THE ANCIENT GREEKS who first developed the *thermae*, but it was the Romans who made the baths their own: sports and leisure centres where it really was possible to cultivate a healthy mind in a healthy body (*mens sana in corpore sano*). The public baths were for rich and poor alike, and no expense was spared – either in the facilities themselves or in the works of art on display: the mosaic pavements, marble walls and statues of heroes.

The Baths of Caracalla, opened in AD 216-17, and covering some 27 acres (11 ha), represented the pinnacle of achievement in Roman bath building. Not only were there baths but also esplanades, a stadium, sitting rooms, libraries and lecture rooms.

Underneath the symmetrically arranged baths lay a network of tunnels, wood-burning furnaces, service quarters and storerooms where the bath attendants and stokers scurried about their business out of sight of the bathers.

Laconicum or Sudatorium
(very hot, dry room)

Palaestra (sports area)

Apodyteria
(changing
rooms)

Natatio (swimming pool)

Main
entrance

RELIGION AND THE AFTERLIFE

All the everyday activities of the Romans – from getting married

to going on a military campaign – were dependent for their

smooth running on the good favours of their gods.

THE ROMANS were a deeply practical people. When it came to military organisation, public administration and civil engineering, they had few rivals in the ancient world. But they were not deep or original thinkers. They did not agonise over the nature of the soul, sin and salvation, or seek to understand the universe or the meaning of life.

They just assumed that these matters were in the hands of the gods and did their best – in practical ways – to secure divine good will in everyday concerns, such as the harvest, health, finance and fertility. As the orator Cicero claimed: 'Jupiter is Best and Greatest not because he makes us just or sober or wise, but because he makes us healthy and right and prosperous.'

As well as a panoply of ancient magic practices, the Romans had a vast array of gods from which to choose. Some of the more ancient ones were no more than spirits associated with a place, such as a wood or river, or with a process – particularly an agricultural one. In addition to these, every family worshipped its own ancestral spirits, the *Lares*, and left offerings of food, wine and incense for them at a shrine in the main room of the house. Every family head also offered prayers and pieces of food to Vesta, the goddess of the hearth, and to the household gods, the *Penates*, who

HOUSEHOLD GOD This bronze statuette of a dancing Lar, a household deity, from Pompeii is typical of the objects of domestic worship in the 1st century AD.

looked after the larder and ensured that there was always enough food at home.

There were further delegations of domestic responsibility to minor gods, such as Limentius who was responsible for the threshold, Cardea for the hinges, and Forculus for the main body of the door. It was exactly this type of divine proliferation that St Augustine mocked in *The City of God*, which he wrote in the 5th century AD: 'How could I possibly record in one passage of this book all the names of the gods and goddesses which the earlier Romans could scarcely enumerate in the huge volumes in which they separated the particular and specific spirits in the environment into individual and distinct categories?'

GODS FROM GREECE

As well as these rather vague and often nameless spirits, the Romans created a pantheon of gods who looked and behaved like humans. They borrowed the characteristics and myths of many of these gods from the Greeks. Jupiter came to resemble the Olympian figure of Zeus, and Juno his wife Hera.

Further adaptations included the Roman Neptune (the Greek Poseidon) and Minerva (Athena), Mars (Ares) and Venus (Aphrodite), Apollo (the same in Roman as Greek) and Diana (Artemis), Vulcan (Hephaestus) and Vesta (Hestia), Mercury (Hermes) and Ceres (Demeter). Each of these gods was responsible for a particular activity: Ceres for growth, Mercury for business, Mars for war (and agriculture), Apollo for healing, Vesta for the hearth, Jupiter for the sky, and so on. The identification between the god and the activity was so complete that people even referred to making love as 'worshipping Venus', and a combination of hunting and studying as 'honouring Diana along with Minerva'. An individual usually singled out for worship

CONCRETE CREATION Dedicated to all the gods, the Pantheon in Rome was one of the finest achievements of Roman architecture. The great vaulted dome, built of concrete, was the widest in the world until the 20th century.

a particular god with whom he had a special affinity: Julius Caesar, for example, was devoted to the goddess Venus, and the emperor Augustus favoured the god Apollo who, he believed, had helped him to win the Battle of Actium.

THE STATE RELIGION

Religion was not simply a private activity, but a public one too. Each Roman legion worshipped a protective deity of its own. Trade associations paid their respects to particular gods: in Ostia, for example, the corn-measurers worshipped Ceres, and the builders Mars. The city of Rome itself sought protection and continued success from Jupiter, and built a temple to the god which presided over the Forum. And, on an imperial scale, emperors from Augustus onwards tried to foster the people's faith in Roma, the spirit of Rome itself, or in those gods, such as Apollo and Mars, who were acknowledged universally. As part of the propaganda, they even had themselves elevated to the status of gods after their death.

Just as the *paterfamilias* offered prayers and sacrifices to propitiate a god on behalf of the family, the public authorities did the same on behalf of the state, when embarking on a military campaign, say, or holding a public assembly. In ancient Rome, there was very little distinction between the spiritual and the secular, and members of the upper class acted as both magistrates and priests. The most senior of the priestly colleges in Rome consisted of the 16 *pontifices,* public officials nominated either by existing members or by the emperor, and then elected by the Senate. In addition to their duties as senior magistrates, these priests advised on all matters of religious observance and looked after the calendar, deciding which

CHURCH AND STATE
A Roman emperor wears the robes of Pontifex Maximus, or chief priest, of the Roman state religion.

GIFT TO THE GODS   A young man makes a burnt offering to the gods.

days were holy and which were not. The leading priest was known as the Pontifex Maximus; he was responsible – among other things – for the religious calendar and for selecting the six Vestal Virgins who tended the eternal fire that burned in the Temple of Vesta, the symbolic hearth of Rome, in the Forum. It was in his capacity as Pontifex Maximus that Julius Caesar was able to reform the calendar, starting the year in January, in a way that has survived until the present day.

Before the coming of Christianity, which offered people a more personal and emotional relationship with their god, the Romans were great believers in

---

SUPREME PONTIFF

One of the titles held to this day by the Roman Catholic Pope is that of Pontifex Maximus. In Rome's pagan past, the chief priest or *pontifex maximus* – literally, 'head bridge-builder' – was responsible for looking after the bridges over the River Tiber.

ritual. It did not matter so much whether the individual was good or bad – since this was determined at birth. But it did matter whether, in conciliating the gods, he or she followed the correct procedures. This could be quite a complicated business.

RITUALS OF DEVOTION

First, you had to choose the god who you believed was most appropriate for the type of help you needed. Then, you had to make sure that you got his or her name and whereabouts right – no easy task when certain Roman gods went under a variety of names, each reflecting a particular function, and lived in a number of different places scattered

DOUBLE-FACED DEITY
A bronze coin depicts the double-headed Janus, the Roman god of doors, gateways and beginnings (the month of January is named after him).

around the Mediterranean. As a result, it was sometimes safer to use a catch-all expression, such as 'whatever name you care to be called' or to address the prayer to 'an unknown god', or to 'the responsible deity' and to throw in, for good measure, the names of a whole

A DAY IN THE LIFE OF
A VIRGIN AT THE TEMPLE OF VESTA

IT WAS THREE in the morning and Claudia, shivering against the winter wind that howled in from the Apennines, wrapped her long white robes more tightly about her. In the hearth of the circular temple, the flame of the goddess Vesta sputtered feebly, as wisps of smoke spiralled towards the hole in the roof.

Claudia, one of six Vestal Virgins selected from Rome's most aristocratic families, knew that if she let the fire die, thereby signalling the imminent destruction of the city of Rome, she would receive a whipping from the Pontifex Maximus. Punishments were generally severe: at least one Vestal Virgin had already been buried alive for violating her vow of chastity. But, mused Claudia, there were

STONE VIRGINS Statues of priestesses now line a courtyard in the House of the Vestal Virgins in the Roman Forum.

privileges to compensate. Next week she was off to the amphitheatre (where special seats were reserved) in a carriage – a privilege shared only with the empress. And, thanks to the allowance provided by the state, she was never short of spending money.

Apart from this freezing night

watch, the other duties of the day to come were relatively light: fetching water from the holy spring, cleaning the temple and decorating it with sprigs of bay and laurel, and preparing the salt cakes used in sacrifices – when she would don a white hood fringed with purple.

Claudia knew that in another 14 years, at the age of 39, her 30 years of service would be up. She would be free to marry and to lead a normal life. But, all in all, as she imagined the elegant courtyard on a warm summer's day, with its marble colonnades and its lily covered pools, and contemplated the vast house with more than 50 rooms, in which she and the other Virgins lived, she thought it just as likely that she would stay on.

LAST RITES AND RESPECTS

FOR THE ROMANS, the rituals that surrounded the mystery of death depended on personal wealth. The poor were simply deposited at night in a common grave, while wealthier citizens were mourned in style and ceremony.

The body of the head of a household was washed and anointed, and laid on a funeral couch in the lamp-lit atrium of his home. It was here that people paid their last respects before accompanying the body to the funeral pyre on the outskirts of the city. Weeping mourners and attendants on this final procession carried wax funeral masks of the deceased and his ancestors.

The Romans shared the Greek belief that dead souls were ferried across the River Styx to Hades, so a coin was often placed in the dead man's mouth to pay the boatman. The body was then cremated on the pyre, and the ashes placed in an urn which was stored, along with provisions for the life beyond, in the family tomb. However, as the Romans came increasingly to crave an afterlife, they began to prefer the idea of burial to cremation. By the 3rd century AD, people looked forward to enjoying the sleep of the dead – whole in body and soul – in their own sarcophagi, surrounded by their own treasured possessions.

FINAL MARCH Musicians lead the funeral procession of a Roman, portrayed reclining on a bier; the dead man's family brings up the rear.

host of other deities. Finally, you had to formulate the prayer – as often as not, a general request for peace, prosperity and health – in such a way as to leave nothing to chance. For example, in one particular prayer from his manual on agriculture, Cato the Elder specifies that he wants Mars to 'prevent, ward off and avert diseases, visible and invisible, barrenness and waste, accident and bad water, that thou wouldest permit the crop and fruit of the earth, the vines and shrubs to wax great and prosper, that thou wouldst preserve the shepherds and their flocks in safety and give prosperity and health to me and our house and household . . .' and so on.

As payment for these divine favours, the supplicants might rely on past acts of devotion to the appropriate god. Alternatively, they might make new gifts of gold and jewellery, or they might perform a sacrifice. Sometimes these offers were made spontaneously – without any suggestion that the god was thereby obliged to answer the prayer. On other occasions, however, the offer was made conditional upon the god's compliance. In the words of one such vow to Jupiter 'If the emperor Titus Caesar Vespasianus Augustus, pontifex maximus, holder of the tribunician power, father of his country, and Caesar Domitian, son of the deified Vespasian of whom we deem that we are speaking, should live and their house be safe on the next 1 January . . . and if you have granted a felicitous issue in the manner that we deem that we are speaking of . . . then we vow that you shall have, in the name of the College of the Arval Brethren, two gilded oxen'.

THE DAY OF THE SACRIFICE

The word sacrifice literally meant to 'make holy', and offerings included any living thing, from flowers and fruit to wine and cereal crops (in the form of sacrificial cakes). More impressive than these

BURNT OFFERING In a mosaic from Sicily, members of a hunting party make a sacrifice to Diana, goddess of hunting.

vegetable offerings, however – and, apparently, more invigorating for the gods – were the sacrifices of living animals.

Whether an individual was making a private sacrifice or public officials were sacrificing an animal on the state's behalf, the temple priests would decide – on the basis of long-standing precedent – what type of animal was most appropriate. Male animals were sacrificed to gods, and female animals to goddesses; white animals were offered to the gods of the heavens, such as Jupiter, and black ones to the gods of the underworld. In the countryside, people might rear their own sacrificial rams, cows, goats, boars, horses and bulls – selecting one of a size appropriate to the occasion. But in town, people would buy an animal in the market, making sure that it was a perfect physical specimen: anything less would displease the gods

SACRIFICIAL SLAUGHTER A bull, a ram and a boar are led to the altar, where a veiled figure – possibly an emperor – officiates.

and make it necessary to begin the ceremony again with a new beast.

On the day of the sacrifice, the supplicant gilded, or attached ribbons to, the horns and tail of the animal, and led it to the temple. The more willingly the animal went to its slaughter, the more likely it was to find favour with the gods. Once arrived, the priests took hold of the beast and presented it at a stone altar at the entrance to the temple, where a fire blazed. Next, they washed their hands in a ritual act of purification, removed the ribbons from the animal's horns and sprinkled sacred flour on its head. The supplicant turned towards the painted statue of the god which stood in a room at the centre of the building and – to the shrill accompaniment of a flautist hired for the occasion – recited his prayer. One of the officials, brandishing a hammer, then knocked the animal on the head

125

so that, dazed, it sank to the ground – whereupon another official slit its throat.

The carcass was then cut up, and the internal organs – liver, heart and kidneys – were checked for any imperfections that might ruin the proceedings. When Emperor Caligula was assassinated in AD 41, people pointed to the fact – without surprise – that an animal he had sacrificed at the start of the year had been missing part of its liver. Specialists known as *haruspices* were sometimes hired to interpret the entrails of sacrificial animals. Assuming

all was well, the meat was cooked on the altar fire for the delectation of the gods, and then eaten by the temple priests and by the family and friends of the supplicant who was hosting the sacrifice.

READING THE SIGNS OF THE FUTURE

The ancient Romans were always wary of embarking on a new enterprise, whether it was some piece of legislation, a military campaign, the inauguration of a public official, or – on a more personal level – a marriage. Before they did so, they would search for

RELIGION AND THE AFTERLIFE

signs from the gods that this was the right time, the right place and, indeed, the right person. Some of them resorted to astrology, which had spread from Asia Minor to Italy in the 2nd century BC and posited that the movement of the heavens dictated everything that happened on earth. But all of them would have been keenly aware of the large role in official Roman religion played by divination, the interpretation of portents.

An individual citizen or a magistrate – in the case of public enterprises – would check the skies for *auspices*, such as thunder, lightning and the way in which birds behaved. The interpretation of many of these signs was relatively straightforward, but in some cases the Romans sought advice from

VILLA OF THE MYSTERIES In suburban Pompeii, there is a villa whose frescoes tell a strange story. Dating from around 60-50 BC, these wall-paintings depict the rites of initiation into the mysteries of the cult of Dionysus. In the centre, a seated priestess prepares for a sacrifice, while to her right, a spirit of the wild plays the lyre.

THE COMFORT OF PHILOSOPHY

In the 1st century BC, many educated people turned to philosophy for comfort and consolation. The Stoics, for example, taught a philosophy that enabled people to live without fear of other men, chance or death. They believed that every individual harbours a spark of that spirit (which they described variously as divinity, nature, reason and fate) which courses through and governs the Universe. For an individual to be in harmony with the spirit of the Universe, he has of his own free will to live in accordance with the nature or reason within himself. Only by being true to himself and his destiny in this way can he free himself of all anxiety.

Prescriptions for rational behaviour included suppressing the emotions and a contempt for worldly vanities. In this respect, the Stoics' ethics of self-discipline and steadfastness were particularly popular with the Romans, even if many of them did not appreciate the philosophical arguments for them. For these were precisely the virtues that the Romans had respected since their earliest history.

If the Stoic believed that it was impossible to live in harmony with nature or reason – either through illness or because he was being forced to do something wrong – he was allowed to commit suicide. In AD 65, Seneca the Younger was ordered to take his own life by his former pupil, Emperor Nero. This ultimate liberation of the soul was exactly the course of action he had applauded as an 'heroic impulse' in others. For example, one man condemned to die in the amphitheatre had found the 'strength necessary to break the chains of human bondage'. Rather than suffer the indignities of such a death and give unworthy pleasure to the spectators,

THE THINKER Seneca the Younger, statesman, lawyer and man of letters, made a major contribution to the Stoic philosophy.

he had pretended to nod his head in sleep as he was being carted off under close guard to the morning show. 'Then he lowered his head until he had stuck it between the spokes of the cartwheel, and remained calmly in his seat until his neck had been broken by the turning wheel.'

---

a type of priest known as an *augur* (distinguished officials such as Cicero and Pliny the Younger were both made augurs). The augurs had catalogued a range of auspices and their significance, distinguishing between the way in which different species of bird sang, flew and alighted. You might, for example, receive a particular sign from a woodpecker, but if an eagle then appeared, this second sign would take precedence.

Taking the auspices (literally 'birdwatching') was a favourite form of divination on military campaigns. The way in which sacred chickens, who had been brought along for the purpose, reacted to food was carefully observed: if the bird gobbled it so greedily that pieces dropped from its beak, all would be well. People misinterpreted these signs at their own peril: the historian Livy tells the story, for example, of the consul Claudius Pulcher who 'took the auspices before a naval battle off Sicily and, finding that the sacred chickens had refused their feed, cried: "If they will not eat, let them drink!" He threw them into the sea, fought the battle in defiance of their warning, and lost it.'

As well as those signs for which people actually

IN ATTENDANCE Two boy attendants in short tunics – one carrying a parasol and the other a basket – give help at a sacrifice.

searched, there was a range of meaningful, unsolicited signs: the crowing of a cock, for instance, in the middle of the night, or a chance remark that someone might ominously have let slip. Finally, there were extraordinary events, such as a cow talking, a statue weeping, earthquakes, blood raining from the heavens, or the Temple of Jupiter being struck by lightning: such prodigies, as they were called, generally meant that something terrible was about to happen.

COUNTRYSIDE SACRIFICE
A spirit of wild life, known as a Silenus, makes a sacrifice at a blazing altar.

ANCIENT OMENS

In his biography of Julius Caesar, Suetonius lists certain events that should have forewarned Caesar of his assassination: a herd of horses shedding bucketfuls of tears; a little bird flying into the Hall of Pompey with a sprig of laurel in its beak only to be torn to pieces by a swarm of different birds in hot pursuit; and a dream in which Caesar himself soared above the clouds and shook hands with the god Jupiter. Even level-headed historians such as Tacitus recognised the importance of such signs. In his account of the suicide of the ill-fated Emperor Otho, who reigned for a few months in AD 69, he mentioned the appearance of an ill-omened bird which vanished only after the emperor's death; and concluded that 'it is undignified, for a historian to invent or collect marvels but I would not presume to discredit the truth of this apparition'.

For help with these troublesome prodigies, the Romans sometimes asked a college of 15 elected public officials to consult the Sibylline Books. During the reign of Augustus, these oracles were kept in the Temple of Apollo on the Palatine Hill, and usually suggested some remedy that might propitiate the gods.

RELIGIONS FROM THE EAST

As their empire spread and they became increasingly influenced by the Hellenic world, many Romans fell under the spell of foreign – often oriental – religions. These involved the worshipper emotionally in a way that the official religion did not. Most of them were founded upon a central myth, in which a god-like figure was resurrected after death, thereby promising an afterlife to initiates. By the 2nd century AD, these cults were coexisting with the more practical, public and passionless gods of the traditional Roman pantheon, who had never made such exclusive promises to a select few.

Some people worshipped Isis, the compassionate Egyptian deity, whose husband Osiris had died and been resurrected. This promise of an afterlife was further reinforced by the fact that, every year, it was the tears of Isis weeping for her drought-stricken land that made the Nile flood and the crops grow again. Other people worshipped Cybele, the Asiatic mother-goddess, whose young lover Attis had also died and been resurrected – an event celebrated each year in a frenzy of ritual devotion, organised by eunuch priests.

From Asia Minor there was Mithras, the bull-slayer and Persian god of light and truth. Popular at first with soldiers (because the cult was confined to men), Mithraism spread rapidly among merchants and civil servants along the trading routes of the Mediterranean world; almost 50 underground shrines, or mithraea, have been found in Rome alone and 18 more in Ostia, dating from the 2nd and 3rd centuries AD. Five shrines have been found in Britain, and it is from the remains of one of these, at the army fort of Carrawburgh in Northumberland, that you can deduce the sort of ceremonies conducted there. On arrival, the 20 or so initiates donned the masks that signified which of the seven grades of initiation they had attained (Raven, Lion, Soldier, Bride, Persian and Father are the six that are known to us today). Initiation into each successive

LIFE BLOOD
Mithras, originally a Persian god, sacrifices a bull whose blood then fertilises the earth.

EYEWITNESS

PERSECUTING THE CHRISTIANS

A GREAT FIRE devastated large areas of Rome in AD 64. Some people blamed Nero for starting the fire. The historian Tacitus describes how the emperor deflected the blame onto the Christians:

● But neither human resources, nor imperial munificence, nor appeasement of the gods, eliminated sinister suspicions that the fire had been instigated. To suppress this rumour, Nero fabricated scapegoats – and punished with every refinement the notoriously depraved Christians (as they were popularly called). Their originator, Christ, had been executed in Tiberius's reign by the governor of Judaea, Pontius Pilate. But in spite of this temporary setback the deadly superstition had broken out afresh, not only in Judaea (where the mischief had started) but even in Rome. All degraded and shameful practices collect and flourish in the capital.

First, Nero had self-acknowledged Christians arrested. Then, on their information, large numbers of others were condemned – not so much for incendiarism as for their antisocial tendencies.

Their deaths were made farcical. Dressed in wild animals' skins, they were torn to pieces by dogs, or crucified, or made into torches to be ignited after dark as substitutes for daylight. Nero provided the Gardens for the spectacle, and exhibited displays in the Circus, at which he mingled with the crowd – or stood in a chariot, dressed as a charioteer. Despite their guilt as Christians, and the ruthless punishment it deserved, the victims were pitied. For it was felt that they were being sacrificed to one man's brutality rather than to the national interest. ●

FOREIGN GOD In a fresco from Herculaneum, priests of the Egyptian goddess Isis perform a religious ceremony.

grade was determined by tests of courage and endurance, all of which took place within the shadowy secrecy of the temple and which included being buried in a pit and covered with stone slabs, branding, torture and the binding together of the postulant's hands with chicken intestines. But the rewards were great: the promise of salvation in the life to come.

It was typical of the Romans to adopt and absorb gods from different parts of their empire – sometimes, in a process known as syncretism, grafting the characteristics of new, foreign gods onto existing

131

THE INTERPRETATION OF DREAMS

THE ROMANS believed firmly in the significance of dreams – to such an extent that the Emperor Augustus, acting on one of his, used to behave like a beggar in the streets of Rome one day a year. Here is a passage from one of the many manuals for interpreting dreams, written by Artemidorus of Ephesus who lived in Rome during the 2nd century AD:

❝ If you dream of a house on fire and it burns with pure flames but does not collapse, it means wealth if you are poor, power if you are rich. But if it is a smoky fire, which destroys the house and brings it down in ruins, it is bad for everyone connected with the house and means the ruin of the owner. If only a part of the house is destroyed, it depends on which part is involved: if it is the bedroom, it means disaster for the wife (or, if there is no wife, for the master of the house); if it is the men's room, it means disaster for all the men of the household; if it is the women's room, for all the women; if it is the storerooms or the housekeeper's room, for the steward or the housekeeper. ❞

Roman ones. Indeed, this principle of the more gods the merrier was one of the Romans' great strengths, as the Christian writer Minucius Felix acknowledged: 'Throughout the whole far-flung empire, in provinces, in towns we see that each local group of people has its own religious rituals and worships local gods. The Eleusinians, for example worship Ceres, the Phrygians worship Great Mother, the Epidaurians Aesculapius, the Chaldeans Baal, the Syrians Astarte, the Taurians Diana, and the Gauls Mercury. The Romans, however, worship all the gods in the world . . . And thus, while the Romans were adopting the religious rites of all nations, they also won for themselves an empire.'

THE COMING OF CHRISTIANITY

In some ways, these new religions – with their stress on personal piety as a means to the soul's salvation in the life to come, and on the worship of a single god who had suffered, died and been buried before rising again – may have paved the way for Christianity. By the reign of the emperor Claudius (AD 41-54), Christianity had spread from Palestine to Rome.

Followers of Christ were to be found at first among the Jewish colony in Rome, where they clashed with the more orthodox supporters of Judaism. The new faith was also popular among slaves and the families of the poor, but its followers were persecuted by the authorities, chiefly because of their refusal to acknowledge any god other than their own. Religion and the Roman state had traditionally been so identified with each other as to be completely inseparable. But the Christians, when questioned about their origins, would say that they were 'Christians' first and foremost, rather than Romans.

Nevertheless, by time of the emperor Hadrian's reign (AD 117-38), many very influential figures had answered the call of Christ. Christianity offered a coherent system of belief, a moral code and a theory of how the world worked (which the cults did not) and a mystical and sacramental dimension (which the philosophical schools did not). By the 4th century AD, Christianity had gained the support of the emperors themselves: in AD 312 the emperor Constantine declared that Christianity was to be officially tolerated, and in AD 392 the emperor Theodosius I – by prohibiting all non-Christian rites – effectively made Christianity the state religion.

HOLY ROMAN Constantine was the first emperor to convert to Christianity.

LIFE IN THE ROMAN EMPIRE

The lush vegetation and exotic animals, including lions, crocodiles and hippopotamuses, to be found along the Nile always exerted a strong fascination for the Romans. But Rome's subject peoples were equally seduced by the peace and prosperity that the Empire brought and by the sophistication of the Roman way of life. They began to emulate Roman values, and to become as Roman as the Romans themselves.

DAILY LIFE OUTSIDE ROME

From Scotland to the edge of the Sahara, and from Spain to Syria, the Roman Empire

was remarkable for its uniformity of language and culture: by the end of the 2nd century AD,

even Britain, a relative backwater, had become a Romanised province.

DESPITE the many ways in which Roman rule changed the everyday lives of its subjects, there were many areas where people continued to speak their native tongues, worship their own gods, and bury their dead in the traditional way. In the mountain areas of northern Africa and Asia Minor, for example; in the desert lands close to the Sahara; along the northern fringes of the empire; or among the Basque people of the Pyrenees, the tribes people would have been almost untouched by Roman civilisation. But, in the main, Roman customs followed in the footsteps of the legions. The network of roads created by the army – first in Italy itself and then in Spain, northern Africa, the Middle East and Asia Minor, France and Germany and finally Britain – formed the conduits along which the Roman lifestyle spread.

THE CONQUEST OF SPAIN AND AFRICA

In 221 BC, as the Carthaginian general Hannibal prepared to launch an invasion of Italy from Spain, the Roman army counter-attacked. It was the start of a series of military campaigns in Spain, which 200 years later, when the last pockets of resistance had been subdued, would leave Rome in complete control of the Iberian peninsula. Another 200 years on, by the end of the 2nd century AD, parts of Spain were as Roman as Rome itself, particularly in the province of Baetica in the south. The Romans established new colonies of veteran soldiers here, but the existing cities soon became miniature models of Rome as well. By the reign of the

emperor Augustus, ten of Baetica's cities had full colonial status and a further 27 were *municipia*, electing their own magistrates and senators, and exercising limited powers of self-government. Their resemblance to Rome was not simply constitutional. With their baths, circuses and theatres, they looked like Rome, too; and, according to the geographer Strabo, people went about dressed in Roman clothes and speaking Latin rather than their native tongues.

During the course of the wars with Carthage in the 2nd century BC, Rome also took control of north-western Africa from the Atlantic to the Gulf of Gabès in Tunisia. It was to rule this coastal strip, which stretches some 1400 miles (2240 km), for more than 500 years. By the 1st century AD, northern Africa – the granary of the Roman Empire – was exporting nearly half a million tons of grain a year. And yet the emperors did not have the government machinery to exploit this great agricultural wealth on their own; as in other areas,

ELEPHANT MAN A coin, showing Hannibal on one side and an elephant on the other, commemorates the great general's crossing of the Alps in 218 BC.

CAPITOLINE TRIAD The Capitoline temple crowns a hill in the Roman city of Thugga (now Dougga) in Tunisia. Dedicated to Jupiter, Juno and Minerva, it was a reminder of the great temple which overlooked the Forum in Rome itself.

SPOILS OF WAR A frieze on the Arch of Titus celebrates the army's triumphal return from Jerusalem in AD 70.

they had to rely on the local people to govern themselves.

Rome's acquisition of Egypt was more gradual. From the middle of the 2nd century BC, Roman influence grew to such an extent that the country effectively became a client state. Eventually it fell under the direct rule of Rome: after the defeat of Antony and Cleopatra at the Battle of Actium in 31 BC, Octavian (soon to be known as the emperor Augustus) 'added Egypt to the empire of the Roman people', as he proudly proclaimed.

Over the next three centuries, Rome brought peace to Egypt. In the cities, particularly the Greek-speaking towns in the Nile Delta or along the Nile itself, the Romans allowed the existing oligarchies to govern themselves much as before – under the

overall control of the Roman prefect. In the countryside, where most people lived in small villages of mud-brick houses made from clay and straw, smallholders and the labourers on the great imperial estates grew grain for export to Rome. Despite the taxes levied by the Romans, these centuries were ones of relative prosperity – the day-to-day fortunes of the rural peasants determined, as ever in Egypt, as much by the level of the Nile as by Roman ownership.

THE MIDDLE EAST AND ASIA MINOR
Rome's acquisition of an eastern empire is similar in its gradual development to what happened in Egypt. In 133 BC, Attalus III, the last of the kings of Pergamum (in modern Turkey) bequeathed his kingdom to his allies, the Roman people. Four years later, it became the first of several Roman provinces in Asia

FOREIGN LEGION This soldier, from Vachères in France, was one of many Gauls who enlisted in the Roman army.

WORTH ONE'S SALT

Salt was one of the earliest commodities traded by man. One of the oldest roads in Italy, the Via Salaria, or Salt Road, linked the salt flats near Ostia to Rome. Our word 'salary' is derived from the salt ration that was distributed as part of a Roman soldier's pay: which is one of the reasons why we describe someone rather ineffective as 'not worth their salt'.

SOLDIER STATESMAN
Among his achievements, the Roman general Pompey subdued Spain, defeated Mithridates in Asia Minor, and subjected Syria and Judaea to Roman authority.

Minor. The ruling hand of the Romans was relatively light, and as in Egypt, the Greek-speaking cities were left very much to govern themselves.

In 63 BC the Roman general Pompey intervened on one side of a family dispute, and his army entered Jerusalem. Herod, a client of the Roman state, was made Governor of Galilee and eventually King of Judaea (later renamed Palestine). So long as he or his son Herod Agrippa were alive, the Romans received their taxes without much trouble; but after the death of Herod Agrippa in AD 44, they were forced to reimpose direct rule. Whereas Herod's new port of Caesarea and the Greek-speaking cities of the coast accepted this and flourished, orthodox Jews rebelled. The revolts culminated in the Jewish War of AD 66, when the zealots took control of Jerusalem. In AD 70 the emperor Vespasian's son Titus recaptured the city.

THE GALLIC WARS

In 58 BC Julius Caesar embarked on seven years of warfare with the Celtic nations of Gaul, at the end of which Rome controlled an area that stretched from the Mediterranean to the English Channel, and from the Atlantic to the Rhine, comprising what are now France, Belgium and Luxembourg, and considerable chunks of the Netherlands, Germany and Switzerland.

The Roman army's greatest achievement, however, probably lay less in its military conquest of Gaul than in its Romanisation of the country. Despite years of exposure to the sight of Roman soldiers and the sound of marching feet, ambitious young Gallic cavalry commanders actually chose to raise and lead their own auxiliary regiments in the service of the Roman army. On retirement, they returned home as Roman citizens, wealthy and well travelled, to rule the tribal areas on behalf of the Empire.

THE INVASION OF BRITAIN

Julius Caesar, who invaded Britain in 54 BC, painted a fairly primitive picture of the country's Celtic tribes people: 'All the Britons dye themselves with woad, and as a result their appearance in battle is all the more daunting. They wear their hair long, and shave all their bodies with the exception of their heads and upper lips. Wives are shared between groups of ten or twelve men, especially between brothers and between fathers and sons.' Despite their bristling moustaches and what might have appeared to the Romans to be barbarian ways, the ancient Britons lived in a relatively sophisticated and prosperous society; some of their decorated metalwork, for instance, was of a very high quality. During the century between the invasion of Julius Caesar and that of AD 43, during the reign of Emperor Claudius, there was considerable trade between south-eastern Britain and the rest of the Roman Empire, particularly Gaul. The geographer Strabo may have decried the Britons' lack of skill

continued on page 140

PRISONERS ON PARADE In this terracotta plaque dating from the 2nd century AD, prisoners from Dacia are paraded through the streets of Rome. They had been captured during Emperor Trajan's campaigns in what is now Romania.

THE ROMAN FORUM

THE ROLE OF THE FORUM, Rome's central meeting place, was replicated in towns throughout the Empire – although, as this reconstruction shows, never on quite the same scale or with such magnificence. The view leads from the roof of the Temple of Divus Julius in the foreground, past the administrative centre of the Basilica Aemilia, on the right, and the law courts of the Basilica Julia on the left. At the far end of the square stand the Arch of Septimius Severus, built in the early 3rd century AD, and the Temple of Concord. Towering above the scene, in the distance on the left, is the Temple of Jupiter Capitolinus. The Temple of the Divus Trajanus is on the right.

Temple of Jupiter Capitolinus

Basilica Julia

Temple of Castor and Pollux

Temple of Divus Julius

Tabularium
(library and public records)

Temple
of Concord

Arch of
Septimius
Severus

Temple of the
Divus Trajanus

Basilica
Aemilia

Via
Sacra

in 'horticulture or farming in general', but his list of British exports included cattle, hides, wheat, gold, silver, iron, slaves and hunting dogs.

As in Gaul, the traditional rulers of Britain were quick to spot the opportunities offered to them by their conquerors. The Romans were equally pragmatic. They may have been ferocious in conquest, but in government they generally adapted to their own advantage what already existed. As a result, rule by the Romans did not necessarily precipitate a revolution in everyday life.

WALL BUILDER A Roman coin, dated AD 132, commemorates Emperor Hadrian, who ordered the building of the wall.

BORDER CONTROL Hadrian's Wall in Northumberland acted as a frontier between Roman Britain and the barbarians beyond. Forts were spaced about a day's march apart – some 14 miles (22 km).

At first glance, the map of the Roman Empire – with the city of Rome in the middle – is a vast swathe of conquered territory. In fact, it was really a conglomeration of thousands of scattered city-states – some consisting of splendid capitals, others of large areas of tribal land. What they all had in common was a desire to emulate Rome itself, both in its manners and in the details of its constitution.

THE ART OF GOVERNMENT

The Romans were essentially an urban people, and could only really conceive of government and society – indeed, of a suitable lifestyle itself – in terms of the city. This was all very well in its Mediterranean territories where – particularly if they had previously been colonised by the Greeks – society already revolved around sophisticated cities. Here, the Romans allowed life to go on much as before.

In other recently conquered territories, veteran soldiers, on being discharged from the army, were granted land in a colony, a new city with a constitution modelled on that of Rome. Examples of these

settlements, which acted as advertisements for the Roman way of life and where the inhabitants were full citizens of Rome, include Narbonne, Arles, Fréjus and Béziers in Gallia Narbonensis; Nyon and Lyons (Lugdunum) in northern Gaul; and Colchester, Lincoln, Gloucester and York in Britain.

So keen were the Romans on governing through a federal network of autonomous city-states that they turned the tribes of their western and north-western provinces into the equivalents of city-states. It did not matter if the territories of, say, the Sequani and the Senones in Gaul, or the Catuvellauni and the Cantiaci in Britain, were considerably bigger than those of the Mediterranean city and did not possess any single settlement that could be described as a capital. At first, these tribal areas, or *civitates*, probably continued to function much as they had done before the conquest. But it was not long before they began to look like Rome and its colonies. The city of Trier in Germany is a fine example of how one of these tribal capitals flourished, particularly in the 2nd and 3rd centuries AD, as a Roman provincial city.

In Britain, the Romans established around ten *civitates* between AD 75 and 90. Each of these tribal areas had its own capital, where councils of the local land-owning aristocracy met to elect the magistrates who administered the community.

The Romans devolved much of the day-to-day administration to these local aristocracies, not from any political principle but in order to shift the burden of collecting taxes and tributes, and maintaining law and order, onto the natives. Roman administration in the provinces could consist quite simply of a governor, with a small official staff, who was in charge of the army and civil administration, and a procurator, responsible for financial matters. In this way, a very few people at the top governed millions of people. You

ANCIENT ARMOUR **Three legionary soldiers (above), their helmets hanging from their shields, decorate a stone relief from a fort on the Antonine Way. The helmet (right) and shield boss (far right) are bronze and have their owners' names stamped onto them.**

only have to look at the letters exchanged between the emperor Trajan and Pliny the Younger, his representative in the province of Bithynia, to appreciate how busy the emperor was with the day-to-day details of government.

So long as the tribes refrained from fighting one another, this hands-off form of government ensured that the existing social structure in the provinces stayed much as before. To that extent, the empire worked in the interests of both the British and the Gallic tribal aristocracy in the 1st century AD. They survived, but dressed up not just in Roman clothing but also in Roman constitutional form.

LIFE IN THE CITY

For wealthy provincials, Roman rule offered as much opportunity as oppression: the chance to govern their own city, to become full Roman citizens, and even to forge careers in the public life of the empire, rising to senator and, in some cases, emperor. They could show off in typically Roman fashion by endowing municipal chairs of grammar and rhetoric, and by providing the money for public entertainments

**ESTATE MANAGEMENT
A landowner checks the accounts of his sharecroppers in a book consisting of five wooden tablets covered with wax.**

and new public buildings. Like their fellow citizens in Rome, they would advertise these benefactions on commemorative inscriptions – in an attempt to attract the gratitude of their colleagues and the attention of the emperor.

In town, they enjoyed the creature comforts of Roman civilisation. They sweated beneath the vast barrel-vaulted ceilings of the public baths, sang along to musical comedies with clowns, mimes and half-naked dancing girls at the theatre, and went as spectators to chariot races and gladiator fights. In many towns, the rituals of everyday life were not that different from those in Rome itself. The Roman peace brought prosperity to the craftsmen and merchants living there, and people traded with the same coins and enjoyed the protection of the same laws. When on official business, the wealthier people in the provinces wore the Roman toga (as the historian Tacitus noted of the British upper classes during the governorship of Agricola around AD 80). And women even followed the fashions in hairstyles favoured by the ladies of the imperial family.

Children in Romanised towns, such as Trier, might be given three names in the Roman style, rather than a single name which remained the norm for most of the population. As part of a deliberate policy of Romanisation, the children of wealthy local aristocrats – whether in Spain, northern Africa, Gaul or Britain – were encouraged to learn Latin, the language of law and public administration, and to receive an education similar to that in Rome. The same children might then train as lawyers, join the army, or attend centres of further education in cities as far apart as Lyons and Ephesus, Alexandria and Trier. When they died, their family might commission – as was the Roman custom – a mausoleum or carved stone monument to commemorate them looking as Roman as possible. As the centuries passed, this practice filtered down from the wealthier aristocrats to craftsmen such as coopers and carriage-makers.

TOWN PLANNING

Not only was the daily routine very similar in many Roman towns but the buildings actually resembled one another, too. When a town was being built from scratch, the surveyors planned it, like the army camp, around two main roads (the *cardo*

LAW AND ORDER IN THE ROMAN EMPIRE

OR ALL ITS MAJESTY, the full arm of Roman law did not always extend into the countryside; and, in its everyday lawlessness, parts of the Roman Empire must have resembled the American Wild West. Brigands ambushed many a traveller, particularly in the malarial Pontine Marshes along the Appian Way, which led from the city of Rome to the heel of Italy. In foreign lands there were barbarian tribes to contend with as well.

Some of these brigands were no more than high-spirited hooligans, as a letter from the future emperor Marcus Aurelius, describing how he and his friends terrorised some shepherds, reveals: 'One shepherd spotted our little group of horsemen and said to the other shepherd, "Keep your eyes on those horsemen, for they often steal and cause great damage." When I heard this, I jabbed my spurs into my horse and galloped him into the middle of the flock. The terrified sheep ran off in all directions, bleating loudly. The shepherd hurled his staff at me . . . the shepherd, who feared to lose his sheep, lost his staff.'

Many cases involved unscrupulous landowners dispossessing weaker – or absent – neighbours by force or chicanery. They might simply invade a neighbour's property with a small private army of slaves, or they might claim that their neighbour had committed suicide and that his estate was therefore liable for confiscation by the imperial treasury, which would then reward the informant with a bonus.

The victim was then faced with a dilemma because, although the Romans had succeeded in replacing arbitrary private justice with

CLAIM FOR DAMAGES Two advocates dispute a lawsuit, which probably involved the broken amphora of oil that lies at their feet.

public justice, Roman law was concerned purely with civil offences. It was up to the person whose farm had been seized to initiate a trial, since the government itself did not prosecute people.

He had to arrest the aggressor himself and bring him physically to court. Next, he had to win his case against an opponent who might have more powerful patrons among the local magistrates. And then even if he won, it was up to him to confiscate for himself goods and chattels to the value of the farm in compensation. In practice, the litigant with the better connections generally won; and, in the absence of a real police force or a penal code, many criminals went unpunished.

Litigation of this sort was really a pastime for the upper classes;

and even then, according to Pliny the Younger, who had practised law since the age of 18, it transgressed natural limits of 'propriety and deference'. Audiences were paid to lend their support to a particular cause – for a fee of around three denarii a case. 'They parley with the contractor,' Pliny continued, 'take the gifts offered on the floor of the court as openly as they would at a dinner party, and move on from case to case for the same sort of pay.'

It is not hard to imagine the noise in, say, the Basilica Julia in Rome where four separate courts, each of which accommodated up to 45 lawyers, partitioned only by flimsy screens, heard civil law cases. Each of these courts also attracted a crowd of booers and cheerleaders.

maximus running from north to south and the *decumanus maximus* running from east to west) that met at right angles in the middle. This is certainly the case with Augst in Switzerland, which was founded in 44 BC, and with Timgad in northern Africa, which was founded as a colony for veteran soldiers and their families in AD 100.

In the army camp or legionary fortress, the junction in the middle was the site of the commander's headquarters. In the town, it was the site of the square or forum, where people gathered to gossip and do business; the *curia* or city hall, where the local senators, or decurions, held their meetings; and the *basilica*, or court of justice. Around these central axes spread the grid pattern of the streets with their houses, craftsmen's workshops and inns.

Few cities followed the perfectly symmetrical street plan of the textbook town. Most developed in a more haphazard way, growing up alongside roads, at river crossings such as Trier (on the Mosel), and beside army forts, such as Chichester and Cirencester in Britain, or along the Rhine frontier which spawned the modern cities of Bonn, Mainz and Strasburg. Nevertheless, most of the buildings themselves were constructed of stone and in the Roman style.

The proud inhabitants of these cities would fill their public spaces with temples, fountains, theatres (as at St Albans and Canterbury), amphitheatres (as at El Djem in northern Africa, which was nearly as large as the Colosseum in Rome), hippodromes (as at Leptis Magna in modern Libya), baths (as at Wroxeter in Shropshire and the massive Barbarathermen at Trier), and monumental arches (as at Colchester and Timgad). They would attempt to outdo neighbouring cities in the scale of their public buildings and the magnificence of the peristyles, mosaics and wall-paintings in their private homes. Water was supplied, as at Rome itself, by aqueducts (the one at Wroxeter could deliver up to 2 million gallons of water a day); and there are still splendid examples to be seen at Segovia in Spain and at Pont du Gard in France.

Although much of the evidence for life in the Roman empire – stone monuments, written records, buildings, and so on – comes from the cities where changes introduced by the Romans were most conspicuous, most subjects of the Empire lived as peasants on the land. They left no record of their lives, but it is safe to assume that their lot was little different from that of their ancestors before the Roman conquest.

LIFE ON THE LAND

In Gaul and Britain, at least three out of four people worked on the land, their horizons stretching no farther than they could see. Here, peasant farmers harvested grain as they had always done; raised sheep, pigs, poultry and cattle; and grew fruit (apples and plums), pulses (peas and beans), root-crops (carrots, parsnips and beets) and vegetables (cabbage and celery). Except for the greater use of iron tools and a heavier plough, which made farming slightly more efficient, the Romans did not introduce any agricultural innovations. As a result, the life of the peasant farmer remained, day in, day out, one of backbreaking toil.

These farmers lived on in the fortified hill-forts, draughty farmsteads or in the roadside hamlets of circular, timber-framed huts that they had occupied before the conquest – with walls of wattle and daub, roofs of thatch, and floors of clay. Their contact with the Roman way of life was determined entirely by the distance they lived from the nearest villa, army fort or market town: the most Romanised areas of the empire therefore included the military zone along the Rhine (the

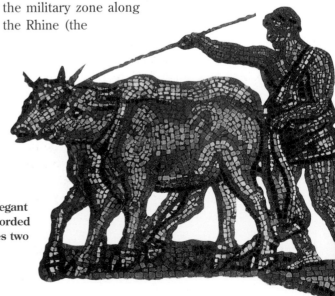

FARMING YEAR The mosaics which decorated an elegant country villa in Saint-Romain-en-Gal, in France, recorded the rhythms of the rural year. Here, a farmer guides two oxen ploughing the light soils of southern France.

frontier between the Empire and the barbarians beyond) and the area around Lugdunum (Lyons), a miniature Rome. By contrast, in the west and north of Britain, where towns and villas were few and far between, the old Celtic ways and language survived the strongest – particularly in Wales and Cornwall. Here, the tribes people continued to live in timber huts within oval settlements known as 'rounds', surrounded by a bank and a ditch. These country folk continued to wear their traditional costumes: the Gauls, for example, sporting an unbelted tunic often with wide sleeves; and the wives of the Ubii tribesmen from Germany wearing a distinctive bonnet on their heads.

COUNTRY WEAR In Roman Europe, agricultural labourers, seen here in front of a rural villa (above) and in a figurine (right), wore a short tunic belted at the waist and a hood which was sometimes allowed to hang down the back.

Much the same was true of life on the land in northern Africa, where the Berber shepherds were distinguished, then as now, by the hooded burnous. Here, only about one person in ten lived in the towns, where Roman influence was strongest; the remaining 90 per cent lived in the countryside as tenant farmers, sharecroppers or landless labourers, working on the great estates and living in straw or mud-walled huts. Whether your landlord or employer was a tribal chief who had kept his land after the conquest, a rich Roman immigrant who had recently been granted some, an army veteran or the emperor himself, life on the land was as hard as ever. Despite the reservoirs and irrigation canals built by the Romans, fluctuations in fortune depended as always on the sun and the seasons, and not on the forces of the Roman Empire. Farther inland, the tribes people led a seminomadic life, growing only enough crops for their own needs. They continued to speak Libyan and to practise ancient rituals, such as burying their dead curled up and painted red.

Life in the countryside did change, however, for wealthier landowners. In Gaul, chieftains who had chosen to fight for the Roman army and had then returned to act as magistrates in the *civitates*, embraced many aspects of the Roman way of life with great enthusiasm. Their descendants built villas in the country, sometimes on the site of existing farmhouses at the centre of their farms, employing anything between ten and a couple of hundred people. Much the same was true of other provinces of the Roman Empire, from the market gardens of southern England to the wheatfields of northern Africa.

THE AGE OF THE VILLA

The Empire's first villas consisted quite simply of a rectangular block, with five or six rooms and a corridor or verandah running along the front. Gradually, these became more sophisticated. By the 3rd and 4th centuries AD – the era of the most energetic villa building – the original rectangular block had sprouted wings on either side, with perhaps a wall or a fourth side linking the two wings and enclosing a central courtyard or garden. Some of these villas were built entirely of brick or stone, instead of traditional timber and wattle and daub, and had tiled roofs rather than thatch. Inside, the plastered walls were graced with paintings reminiscent of Herculaneum and Pompeii; and the floors sparkled with glorious mosaics. The Romans had even developed a form of domestic central heating, which maintained the temperature of certain rooms at

TREASURE TROVE **This silver platter formed part of the hoard unearthed at Mildenhall in Suffolk in 1942.**

around 21°C (70°F), and which was – amazingly – ignored by the civilisations which followed over the next 1500 years. The system consisted of a wood or charcoal-fired furnace which pumped hot air along channels beneath some of the ground-floor rooms, while flues hidden behind the walls conducted heat along the sides of the room. With its underfloor heating and drainage systems, the Roman villa was a far cry from the Iron Age hut house with its two or three all-purpose rooms.

In northern Africa too, in the 4th and 5th centuries AD, the rich moved away from the towns to similar villas on their country estates. As can be seen in the mosaics depicting life in the African villa, the verandah running the full length of the front provided some shade; behind that stretched a complex of stables and barns, bathhouses and pleasure gardens.

In 1942 a farmer, ploughing a field at Mildenhall in Suffolk, turned up a total of 34 pieces of ornamental silver – dishes, bowls, spoons and chalices. This extraordinary treasure trove had probably once belonged to a wealthy East Anglian landowner, and is some indication of the luxurious lifestyle and expensive tastes enjoyed by the most fashionable families living in Roman Britain in the 4th century AD. Such people could quaff wine produced on a Greek island from a glass vessel made in Syria, and eat Colchester oysters or Italian figs off a silver dinner-service manufactured in the south of France. Those who could not quite afford silver dined off samian pots or bronze from Gaul and Italy. A similarly wealthy lifestyle is typical of Gaul, where archaeological finds, including the jewellery and furniture of the rich, illustrate the growth in prosperity that Roman rule brought to the country.

TRANSPORT AND TRADE

Trade flourished under the Romans – encouraged by a better transport system that linked town and country, consumers and producers. Before the

ROAD SIGN **A weary traveller plods with his donkey along a Roman road, marked at intervals of 1000 paces by a stone.**

arrival of the Romans, most European societies had traded along rivers such as the Danube and the Durance, the Guadalquivir and the Garonne, rather than along roads. By the 4th century AD, however, there were some 53 000 miles (85 000 km) of road connecting the city of Rome with the most far-flung provinces of its empire. In northern Africa alone, a road ran 2800 miles (4480 km) along the coast from Tangiers to Alexandria, from where it extended into the Middle East. And in Britain, where there had been no roads worthy of the name before the Roman conquest, archaeologists have now traced more than 6000 miles (9600 km) of major Roman roads – principal among them Watling Street, Fosse Way, and Ermine Street which ran from London to Scotland. Complete with milestones and inns, where the messengers of the imperial postal service could rest, these closely resembled the highways of Italy itself. The Roman genius for engineering extended to bridges: for example, across the Danube in Romania, across the Rhine in Germany, and at Alcantara where a bridge linking Spain and Portugal straddles a gorge 600 ft (180 m) wide, 200 ft (60 m) above the River Tagus.

In a major port such as London, where wharves stretched a good half-mile along the waterfront, goods from all the provinces of the empire were constantly being exchanged. British

'GREATER AND MORE NECESSARY MATTERS'

WATER SUPPLY   The Pont du Gard, a Roman aqueduct, carried water to the city of Nîmes in southern France.

THE ROMANS directed their practical genius at many of the problems of everyday life in the city: particularly at the supply of water and the disposal of sewage. In a passage from his *Geography Book*, the Greek historian and geographer Strabo (*c*.63 BC–AD 24) praises their engineering achievements:

❛ To the blessings which nature has bestowed upon their city the Romans have added others which can be attributed to their foresight. For the Greeks were renowned for their successful endeavours in the area of city planning because they sought out locations which were naturally beautiful, and also easily defended, which had harbours and also rich soil.

The Romans however were especially farsighted about matters to which the Greeks gave little thought, such as the construction of roads and aqueducts, and of sewers which could wash out the waste matter of the city into the Tiber. They have constructed roads throughout the countryside, cutting through hills and filling in depressions, so that now their wagons can carry loads equivalent to those of boats. The sewers, covered with a vault of tightly fitted stones, have room in some places for hay wagons to drive through them. And the quantity of water brought into the city by aqueducts is so great that rivers, as it were, flow through the city and the sewers; and almost every house has water tanks, service pipes, and plentiful streams of water . . . In short, the ancient Romans gave little thought to the beauty of Rome because they were occupied with other, greater and more necessary matters. ❜

MILITARY ENGINEER
The Roman emperor, Trajan supervises the building of a fortified bridgehead during his conquest of Romania.

MONEY ECONOMY   **Under the Romans, money became a common medium of exchange throughout the Empire.**

woollen coats were exported to Gaul and the Rhineland, and lead to distant Pompeii; while imports included glossy red samian-ware pots manufactured in Gaul (at peak production, the workshops of La Graufesenque and Lezoux were turning out millions of vessels a year). Similar patterns were repeated throughout the empire; goods manufactured in Italy have been found as far afield as Scandinavia, and there were even trading connections with India and China. Processes were traded as well as products; for example, the art of glass-blowing (first practised in Syria in the 1st century BC) soon spread to workshops in northern France.

One of the forces driving this booming economy was the Roman army. Its presence on the Rhine created a permanent market for food and clothing, most of which was supplied by Gaul. Similarly, in Britain, the army boosted demand for grain, for metals such as gold, silver, lead, copper, iron and tin, and for pottery produced in the workshops of the New Forest or the Nene Valley, which eventually eclipsed the imported pottery.

These goods were paid for in Roman coins by the cash-rich soldiers and officials of the Empire. In turn, the native farmers and craftsmen of the conquered territories acquired desirable Roman goods; and a money economy of some sophistication soon developed. Public-building programmes in the towns, and the spate of private villa-building in the countryside, stimulated the quarrying and production of a whole range of construction materials: flint and chalk in the south-east of Britain, for

example; Purbeck marble from Dorset; slate from Leicestershire; and limestone from the Cotswolds. The building of Cirencester alone may have taken around 18 million cubic ft (500 000 m³) of stone – enough to have built nearly half of Hadrian's Wall. There was a similar building boom in northern Africa where, by the 3rd century AD, there were some 600 cities.

THE MOVEMENT OF PEOPLE

People moved around the empire almost as freely as goods. Craftsmen travelled wherever their particular skills were most in demand. Of the 50 000 or so Roman soldiers stationed in Britain, many of them came not from Italy itself, but from northern Africa, Spain, France, Germany, eastern Europe, Greece, Turkey and Syria.

There was little evidence of racial discrimination in the Empire; indeed, one of the most extraordinary features of Rome's ability to assimilate different peoples was the cosmopolitan character of its emperors. Towards the end of the 1st century AD, people from the provinces were becoming increasingly influential. Distinguished Spaniards included the poet Martial, the philosopher Seneca, the rhetorician Quintilian and, of course, Trajan who became the first provincial emperor in AD 98 and was himself succeeded by a compatriot, Hadrian, in AD 117.

Next came the orators and advocates from North Africa, who dominated public life in the later 2nd century. By AD 190, almost a third of Rome's senators were of African origin, and Africans had also infiltrated other areas of everyday life, forging careers in trade, shipping and the army. Most distinguished of all was the first of the African emperors, Septimius Severus, who was born in Leptis Magna in AD 145, and was recognised as emperor in AD 193. His career is typical of many Roman high-flyers – for its wide range of different regions. From AD 170, when the 25-year-old Septimius Severus entered the Senate, he served, among many other appointments, as legate in Africa, deputy head of the civilian administration of northern Spain, commander of a legion in Syria, proconsul of Sicily, and governor of Upper Pannonia on the Danube. He died as emperor in AD 211 in York – several thousand miles from his birthplace – after three years of battling against the Scots.

In the 3rd century, power passed to men with Syrian connections, such as the emperor Elagabalus (AD 218–22).

Religion in the Roman Empire

The Romans were remarkably tolerant of the religions professed by their subjects. They may have suppressed the Druid priests in Gaul with great ferocity, but they did so because they considered them a focus for political resistance. In most areas, however, people continued to worship their local gods, often in association with an imported Roman deity, such as Mars, Minerva or Mercury. The Romans were adept at identifying a local cult with one of their own; so, for example, the Roman god of war was linked with the Gallic god of light to produce Mars Loucetius, and with the chief god of the Treveri, who lived around Trier, to produce Mars Lenus. This fusion of Classical and Celtic deities achieved (literally) concrete expression in the Romano-Celtic temples. Dedicated to multicultural gods, such as Mars Lenus, many of these were built over the remains of earlier Iron Age sanctuaries; yet the architecture, or at least the colonnaded

WINTER WORK Peasants in Gaul press olives – a task usually carried out in December.

façade, was decidedly Roman. In northern Africa, too – at the same time as the city-dwelling Africans were giving themselves Roman-sounding names – their chief god, Baal-Hammon, was sometimes worshipped as Saturn or as the top Roman god, Jupiter.

Holy places, such as wells, springs, groves and rivers, played as much of a part in ancient African or Celtic religion as they did in Roman religion. As a result, towns such as Bath or Buxton in England – with their healing springs – continued to be just as popular during the Roman occupation as they had been before. In Bath, Sulis, the Celtic goddess of the springs, was linked with Minerva, the Roman goddess of healing, to create Sulis Minerva.

The conquered peoples also took to the Roman gods, particularly in public. For a wealthy community to build and dedicate a temple to one of the gods of the Roman pantheon was a very obvious way of signalling acceptance of Roman civilisation. From Dougga in Tunisia to Augst in Switzerland, there were temples to the triad of gods who graced the Capitoline Hill in Rome: Jupiter Optimus Maximus ('the best and greatest'), his consort Juno, and Minerva. The native peoples even worshipped the spirit of Roma Aeterna and the imperial cult – for example, at the great altar just outside Lugdunum (Lyons) which was dedicated in 12 BC to Rome and Augustus, or at the temple of the emperor Claudius in Colchester in Britain.

In much the same way as its citizens travelled without let or hindrance across the empire, so there was a constant to-ing and fro-ing of ideas and beliefs. Rome exported many of its own gods to its western provinces, but it also imported many oriental gods from its eastern provinces. These then spread right across the empire: Cybele and Attis from Asia Minor; Isis and Serapis from Egypt; and Mithras, the Persian god of light whom the Roman army transported as far west as Britain. The spread of Christianity through the empire was to be even more dramatic.

TIME CHART

POLITICAL HISTORY OF ROME

753 BC According to legend, the city of Rome is founded.

c.509 BC Rome's last king, Tarquinius Superbus (Tarquin the Proud), is expelled. Rome is declared a republic.

c.494 BC In protest at the policies of the patrician governing class, a number of plebeians secede or 'retire' from the rest of the Roman community. As a result, they win the right to elect tribunes to protect the interests of the people.

c.476 BC Some 300 members of Rome's ruling clan, the Fabii, are killed in battle with the Etruscans.

471 BC A plebeian council is established.

445 BC Patricians and plebeians are permitted by law to intermarry.

OLD TOWN Some of Rome's earliest buildings.

439 BC After a plebeian revolt in Rome, Lucius Quinctius Cincinnatus is appointed dictator.

CHRONOLOGY OF EVERYDAY LIFE

c.600 BC Rome's massive sewer, the *Cloaca Maxima*, is built; it runs from the Forum to the Tiber and is still in use 2500 years later.

509 BC Work on the Temple of Jupiter on the Capitoline Hill is completed.

498 BC The first Temple of Saturn in Rome is built.

484 BC Building of the Temple of Castor and Pollux in Rome.

451-450 BC Roman laws are codified into a form known as the Twelve Tables.

SEWAGE SYSTEM
The stone face of a river god is said to mark one of the manholes in Rome's sewer.

431 BC Building of the Temple of Apollo in Rome; it later housed Greek art.

ROME IN RUINS Three columns are all that remains of the Temple of Castor and Pollux.

ROME AND THE REST OF THE WORLD

800-700 BC Greeks settle on the coast of Spain, in southern Italy and in Sicily.

800-700 BC The prophet Isaiah teaches the coming of the Messiah.

800-700 BC Building of the royal palace at Nineveh begins.

776 BC First recorded Olympic Games, featuring wrestling, boxing, horse-racing, running and pentathlon; women are not admitted as spectators.

700-600 BC Assyrians, at the height of their empire, destroy Babylon, Memphis and Thebes. They are, in turn, defeated by the Medes, Babylonians and Scythians.

EASTERN EMPIRE Assyrian soldiers on the march, armed with bows and arrows.

GLORY OF GREECE   The Parthenon was consecrated in 438 BC.

700-600 BC Work starts on the Acropolis in Athens.

700-600 BC Greeks found Paestum in southern Italy and Massilia (Marseilles) in France.

c.640 BC Birth of Solon (dies 560 BC), the Athenian statesman and lawgiver.

600-500 BC Mayan civilisation in Mexico dates from this period.

600-500 BC Building of the theatre at Delphi.

600-500 BC Some of the Old Testament is written during the Babylonian Captivity of the Jews.

600-500 BC Building of the Temple of Artemis at Ephesus, one of the seven wonders of the ancient world.

600-500 BC Nebuchadnezzar II builds a palace at Babylon with terraced gardens ('Hanging Gardens'), another of the seven wonders of the ancient world.

c.563-483 BC Life of Gautama Buddha; in 521 he preaches his first sermon in the deer park of the holy city of Benares.

553 BC Reign of Cyrus II of Persia (dies 529 BC) begins. He conquers Lydia, the Medes and Babylonia, transforming Persia into a vast empire.

c.551-479 BC Life of Confucius.

500 BC Birth of Pericles (dies 429 BC), the Athenian general and statesman. The Periclean Age in Athens is the age of philosophers, poets, playwrights and historians.

490-449 BC Persian Wars between the Greeks and the Persians.

431-404 BC The Peloponnesian War is fought between Athens and Sparta.

400 – 201 BC

CITY WALLS Many stretches of the Servian Walls are still visible today.

c.390 BC Gauls from northern Italy capture and sack Rome before withdrawing. The city is rebuilt, and in 378 BC the Romans erect massive new city walls, known misleadingly as the 'Wall of Servius Tullius'.

366 BC Rome's first plebeian consul is elected.

339 BC The Publilian Laws decrees that one of Rome's consuls must be a plebeian.

300 BC Roman plebeians are allowed to become priests for the first time.

297 BC The Hortensian Law states that the resolutions of the plebeian council should have the force of law.

287 BC Plebeians are awarded equal rights with patricians in Rome.

232 BC The Flaminian Land Law distributes land to ex-soldiers.

---

366 BC Building of the Temple of Concordia in Rome.

338 BC First Roman coins appear. The denarius appears.

312 BC Work begins on the Via Appia (Appian Way), running 132 miles (211 km) from Rome to Capua. It is extended to Brindisi in about 272 BC.

269 BC Romans establish their first mint in the Temple of Juno Moneta – the origin of our word 'money'.

264 BC The first public gladiatorial combats are staged in Rome.

263 BC A sundial is brought from Sicily to Rome.

240 BC Comedies of Livius Andronicus first performed in Rome. Over the next 100 years, plays of Plautus and Terence also become popular.

c.220 BC The Flaminian Way, stretching from Rome to Rimini, is under construction.

CLASSICAL COMEDY In a scene from a comedy by Plautus, thieves try to drag a miser off his money chest.

---

400 BC Carthaginians occupy Malta; in 396 BC they destroy Messina.

396 BC After a ten-year siege, Romans capture the Etruscan city of Veii.

359-336 BC Philip II of Macedon establishes Macedonian power over Greece.

343-341 BC First Samnite War between Romans and the Samnites, warlike peasants from the Apennines.

338 BC Campania is incorporated into the Roman state. Over the next 75 years or so, Rome expands until it controls by colonisation, conquest or alliance all of Italy south of the Po.

CAVALRY KING The king of Macedonia, Philip II.

WALL BUILDER The Chinese emperor Shi Huang Di ordered the building of the Great Wall in the 3rd century BC.

336 BC Philip of Macedon is succeeded by Alexander the Great.

327-304 BC Second Samnite War.

298-290 BC Third Samnite War, which ends with the final subjection of the Samnites and Umbrians.

289 BC The Senones, a Gaulish tribe, defeat the Romans at Arretium.

280-275 BC Pyrrhus of Epirus, a Greek ruler, crosses into southern Italy to help the Greek cities against Rome. He is defeated, and now Rome's power extends throughout Italy.

264-241 BC First Punic War between Rome and Carthage.

238 BC Sardinia and Corsica are occupied by the Romans.

228 BC Hasdrubal founds the city of Carthago Nova (Cartagena).

227 BC Sicily and Sardinia are made provinces of the Roman Empire.

225 BC Romans defeat the Gauls and, three years later, cross the Po to conquer northern Italy.

219-201 BC Second Punic War. In 218 BC the Carthaginian general, Hannibal, crosses the Alps and defeats the Romans at Lake Trasimene (217 BC). The following year, the Romans are defeated again at the battle of Cannae and, by 211, the Carthaginians are almost at the the gates of Rome itself. However, between 211 BC and 206 BC, the Roman general Scipio Africanus defeats the Carthaginians in Spain and, in 202 BC, beats Hannibal at Zama in northern Africa; this effectively brings the war to an end. For the next 70 years, the Romans are at war in Spain.

215 BC Great Wall of China is constructed in order to keep out foreign invaders.

202-191 BC Romans conquer Cisalpine Gaul.

200 – 51 BC

POLITICAL HISTORY OF ROME

133-123 BC Tiberius and Gaius Gracchus, the young tribunes of the people, introduce land law reforms.

101 BC Marius, the man who reorganised the Roman army on a semi-professional basis, defeats the two tribes who had formed an alliance to invade Italy: the Teutones at the Battle of Aquae Sextiae; and the Cimbri at Vercellae.

100 BC Birth of Gaius Julius Caesar (dies 44 BC).

90-87 BC Civil war

ARMY REFORMER The successful Republican general, Marius.

between Rome and her Italian allies, known as the Social War. Sulla, the Roman general and leader of the aristocratic conservative party, expels the popular democratic leader Marius; gains control of Italy (89 BC); seizes Rome (87 BC); and is made dictator for life (82 BC). He resigns the dictatorship in 80 BC and dies in 78 BC.

89 BC The government of Rome grants full Roman citizenship to all free people in Italy.

70 BC Consulships of Pompey and Crassus.

63 BC Birth of Gaius Octavius (the future Roman emperor Augustus).

63 BC Consulship of Cicero.

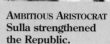

AMBITIOUS ARISTOCRAT Sulla strengthened the Republic.

60 BC Caesar forms the first triumvirate with Pompey and Crassus, and is made consul in 59 BC; Crassus is killed by the Parthians at the Battle of Carrhae in 53 BC.

CHRONOLOGY OF EVERYDAY LIFE

c.200 BC Cato the Elder writes his manual on farming, *De agricultura*. Some five years later, he is elected consul.

179 BC The Aemilian Bridge and the Basilica Aemilia are built in Rome.

167 BC Direct taxation of Roman citizens is abolished.

c.159 BC The first water clock appears in Rome.

150 BC Romans discover that volcanic dust from Pozzuoli, near Vesuvius, when mixed with lime and water, sets hard to create a material which they called *caementum* – forerunner of modern cement. Elsewhere the Romans made a similar material by mixing clay,

limestone and gypsum; when gravel, crushed stone, sand and water were added, the mixture set as hard as natural stone. Concrete enabled the Romans to build their system of roads, sewers and aqueducts.

c.95 BC Birth of the Roman poet Lucretius (dies *c*.55 BC). Other great poets born over the next 50 years include Catullus (84-54 BC), Virgil (70-19 BC), Horace (65-8 BC) and Ovid (43 BC - AD 18).

LOVE POET Ovid still influences literature.

90 BC The Greek physician, Asclepiades of Bithynia, practises in Rome: he was an advocate of dietetics.

79 BC The first cherry trees are brought to Rome from Asia Minor by Lucullus.

63 BC A system of shorthand is devised by the freed Roman slave Marcus Tullius Tiro for recording the speeches of the orator Cicero. *De oratore* is published in 55 BC and *De republica* in 51 BC.

58 BC Roman citizens are entitled by law to receive free public grain.

55 BC Pompey's theatre is completed.

ROME AND THE REST OF THE WORLD

200-100 BC Earliest evidence of paper, found in a tomb in China.

171-167 BC Third Macedonian War, between Rome and Macedonia, ends with the defeat of Perseus by the Romans at the Battle of Pydna.

150 BC The screw press is used by the Greeks to extract grape juice and olive oil.

149-146 BC Third Punic War. Romans destroy Carthage and Corinth in 146 BC.

CITYSCAPE In 63 BC Pompey captured the city of Jerusalem, shown here in a mosaic.

147 BC Rome annexes Macedonia. Greece falls under Rome's dominion.

136-132 BC First slave rising in Sicily.

133 BC Attalus of Pergamum bequeaths his kingdom to the Roman people; in 129 BC Asia Minor becomes Rome's eighth province (along with Sicily, Sardinia and Corsica, the two Spains, Gallia Transalpina, Africa and Macedonia).

121 BC Gallia Narbonensis becomes a Roman province.

104-102 BC Second slave rising in Sicily.

73-71 BC Spartacus leads a slave revolt in Sicily; this is put down by Pompey and Crassus.

66-63 BC Pompey defeats Mithridates VI, King of Pontus, and reorganises the East. In 63 BC Pompey invades Syria and completes the conquest of Palestine, capturing Jerusalem. This signals the end of the independent kingdom of Judaea.

58-49 BC Caesar conquers Gaul and invades Britain (55-54 BC).

50 BC – AD 50

49 BC Caesar crosses the River Rubicon and starts Civil War with Pompey for control of Rome. He defeats Pompey at the Battle of Pharsalus in 48 BC (Pompey is murdered in Egypt the following year).

44 BC On March 15, Caesar is murdered by a group of conspirators led by Brutus and Cassius. A second triumvirate – Antony, Lepidus and Octavian, Caesar's nephew and heir – takes over.

42 BC At the Battle of Philippi, the triumvirs defeat Brutus and Cassius, who commit suicide afterwards.

36 BC Octavian eliminates Sextus

Pompeius, the son of Pompey, and Lepidus.

27 BC Octavian is renamed Augustus and becomes the first emperor of Rome until his death in AD 14.

AD 14 Tiberius succeeds Augustus.

AD 37 Caligula succeeds Tiberius as emperor, but is assassinated by the Praetorian Guard in AD 41.

AD 41 Claudius succeeds Caligula.

VICTORY GIFT Augustus (seated) receives a statuette of victory from Tiberius.

46 BC Work begins on the new (Julian) forum in Rome.

46 BC Julius Caesar modifies the Egyptian calendar to create the Julian calendar – 365 days a year and a leap year of 366 days every fourth year.

18 BC Augustus reforms the marriage laws. Other innovations include the world's first firefighting forces (Rome had at least seven fire brigades, whose members fought blazes using crude water pumps and blankets soaked in vinegar) and passports. Passes granting safe conduct were issued as early as the reign of Augustus. Their wording ran: 'If there be anyone on land or sea hardy enough to molest this traveller, let him consider whether he be strong enough to wage war with Caesar.'

13-11 BC Construction of the Theatre of Marcellus.

10 BC First clear description of the crane by Vitruvius, although Archimedes in the 3rd century BC is said to have devised a crane with three pulleys. The Romans used treadmills – huge wheels inside which slaves walked around to power the crane.

4 BC Birth of philosopher and statesman, Lucius Annaeus Seneca the Younger (he commits suicide on the orders of his former pupil, the emperor Nero, in AD 65).

2 BC Forum of Augustus dedicated.

AD 3 Maison Carrée, a temple, is built at Nîmes.

AD 8 Death of the poet Horace (born 65 BC), author of satires, odes and *The Art of Poetry*.

c.AD 40 Birth of the poet Martial (dies *c.* AD 104). A Spaniard by birth, Marcus Valerius Martialis was the writer of a series of brilliant epigrams which are a great source of information on everyday life in ancient Rome.

CHANGE OF STATE Octavian, later Augustus, rebuilt the Roman state.

47 BC Herod appointed governor of Galilee; in 37 BC he is made King of Judaea.

47 BC The Library of Ptolemy I in Alexandria is destroyed by fire.

46 BC Northern Africa becomes a Roman province.

34 BC Dalmatia becomes a Roman province.

31 BC Octavian and

Agrippa defeat Antony, who had returned to Egypt in 38 BC, and his mistress Cleopatra, the last Queen of Egypt, at the Battle of Actium. Egypt becomes a Roman province in 30 BC.

27-19 BC Agrippa completes the conquest of north-west Spain.

c.5 BC Birth of Jesus Christ.

AD 6 Rome takes control of Judaea, which becomes a Roman province.

AD 30 Crucifixion of Jesus Christ.

AD 43 During Claudius's reign, Romans invade Britain under Aulus Plautius.

CHRISTIAN TIMES Jesus Christ, depicted in a Roman catacomb.

CHRIST CRUCIFIED An ivory shows a scene from Christ's Passion.

AD 51 – 150

POLITICAL HISTORY OF ROME

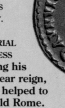

IMPERIAL BUST This cameo, in agate, portrays the Emperor Claudius.

AD 54 Emperor Claudius is poisoned by his wife Agrippina. Her son Nero becomes emperor in his place but he has Agrippina killed in AD 59.

AD 67 Execution of St Peter.

AD 68-9 Nero commits suicide; Galba, and then Otho and Vitellius succeed Nero as emperor.

AD 69 'Year of the four emperors' as Vespasian succeeds Vitellius as emperor.

AD 79 Titus succeeds Vespasian as emperor.

AD 81 Domitian succeeds Titus as emperor. Work begins on Domitian's palace on the Palatine Hill.

EVIL EMPEROR Emperor Nero ordered the murder of both his mother and his wife.

AD 96 Nerva succeeds Domitian as emperor.

AD 98 Trajan succeeds Nerva.

AD 117 Hadrian succeeds Trajan as emperor.

AD 138 Antoninus Pius succeeds Hadrian as emperor.

IMPERIAL SUCCESS During his two-year reign, Titus helped to rebuild Rome.

CHRONOLOGY OF EVERYDAY LIFE

c.AD 61 Birth of Pliny the Younger, lawyer, administrator and landowner (dies *c.* AD 113).

AD 64 Nero launches the first wave of persecutions against the Christians.

AD 64 A great fire devastates Rome.

AD 79 Mount Vesuvius erupts, burying Pompeii and Herculaneum in southern Italy. Bronze drawing compasses dating from this year have been found at Pompeii.

AD 80 Inauguration of the Colosseum in Rome.

AD 81 Arch of Titus erected in Rome.

AD 112-13 The Forum of Trajan and Trajan's Column are dedicated.

SURVIVING STATUE The statue of Apollo stands in front of the ruined Temple of Apollo in Pompeii.

AD 125 One of the earliest uses of the dome – in the building of the Pantheon in Rome, the largest dome in the world until the 20th century.

AD 122-35 Hadrian's Wall is built in Britain, as a defence against the tribes of Scotland.

AD 130 Fulling – a process for cleaning and thickening wool prior to spinning – is thought to have been devised during the Roman occupation of Greece.

c.AD 150 The first recognisably modern guidebook – with descriptions of temples, battlefields and historical sites – is written by the Greek writer Pausanias for people touring Greece.

ROME AND THE REST OF THE WORLD

COMMEMORATIVE COIN A coin celebrates the capture of Jerusalem.

AD 61 Rising of the Iceni under Boudicca (Boadicea) in Britain.

AD 66-73 Jews rebel against the Romans; in AD 70. Romans recapture and destroy Jerusalem; Masada falls in AD 73.

AD 78-84 Agricola's campaigns in Britain.

AD 101-102 First Dacian War.

AD 105-106 Second Dacian War, at the end of which Rome annexes Dacia (modern Romania).

AD 114-17 Trajan's campaigns in Parthia: Armenia and Mesopotamia are annexed.

AD 132-35 Hadrian puts down the Second Jewish Revolt.

PEACE TALKS In a scene from Trajan's Column, the emperor negotiates with the defeated Dacians.

AD 151 – 550

AD 161 Marcus Aurelius succeeds Antoninus Pius as emperor.

AD 180 Commodus succeeds his father as emperor.

AD 192 Commodus is murdered and is succeeded by Septimius Severus (AD 193), who rebuilds his home town of Leptis Magna.

AD 211 Septimius Severus dies and is

HOMAGE **Barbarian chiefs honour Marcus Aurelius.**

SOLDIER KING **Caracalla** (AD 188-217).

succeeded by his sons Caracalla and Geta; Caracalla murders Geta.

AD 217 Caracalla assassinated; he is succeeded by Heliogabalus.

AD 222 Alexander Severus succeeds Heliogabalus.

AD 235 Maximinus succeeds Alexander Severus as emperor.

AD 238 Maximinus is murdered by his own troops and is succeeded by Gordian I and Gordian II, Balbinus, Pupienus and Gordian III.

AD 244 Philip the Arabian succeeds Gordian III as emperor.

AD 249 Decius succeeds Gordian III.

AD 251 Gallus succeeds Decius.

AD 270-75 Reign of Aurelian. He defeats the Marcomanni and Alemanni; builds new walls in Rome in AD 271.

AD 284-305 Reign of Diocletian.

AD 301 Diocletian's Edict on Prices.

AD 162 The physician Galen travels to Rome and wins immediate renown; in AD 169 he is appointed court physician by Marcus Aurelius.

AD165-80 A great plague, probably picked up by Roman soldiers in Mesopotamia, ravages Rome and its empire.

DEADLY GAMES **Gladiatorial contests were popular until the 4th century AD.**

AD 193 The Column of Marcus Aurelius in Rome is completed.

AD 212 Emperor Caracalla grants Roman citizenship to all freeborn subjects of the Roman Empire.

AD 212-17 Building of the Baths of Caracalla.

AD 248 Millenary Games held in Rome to celebrate the city's 1000th birthday.

AD 251-3 A major plague epidemic.

AD 313 Constantine publishes the Edict of Milan, which brings to an end the persecution of Christians in Rome.

AD 313-22 Rome's first Christian basilica is built.

AD 325 Constantine bans public gladiatorial contests.

AD 362 First public hospital for the sick is established in Rome by Julian.

c.AD 540 During the reign of Justinian, the Eastern Emperor, the Digest of Roman Law is compiled.

TRIUMPHAL ARCH **The Arch of Constantine was the largest one to be erected in Rome.**

AD 220 Goths invade Asia Minor and the Balkan Peninsula.

AD 257 Goths invade the area around the Black Sea. In AD 268 they sack Athens, Sparta and Corinth.

AD 293 Roman Empire partitioned into Western and Eastern Empires, with two emperors.

AD 306 Constantine the Great becomes emperor and, in AD 323, reunites the two halves of the Roman Empire under his sole authority, with Byzantium (Constantinople) the capital.

AD 340 The Roman Empire splits in two again.

AD 383 Roman legions start to leave Britain; the last troops leave in AD 436.

AD 401-450 Barbarians take over large areas of the Roman Empire: Vandals and Visigoths in Spain, Huns in Pannonia, Ostrogoths in Dalmatia, Vandals in northern Africa, Franks in Gaul, and Saxons, Jutes and Angles in Britain.

AD 401 Visigoths invade Italy.

HARBOUR SCENE **A mosaic depicts the port at Ravenna.**

AD 404 Ravenna becomes the capital of the Western Empire.

AD 410 Alaric, the king of the Visigoths, sacks Rome.

AD 455 Vandals sack Rome.

AD 476 The Western Roman Empire comes to an end, as the German Odoacer deposes the last Roman emperor.

ACKNOWLEDGMENTS

ABBREVIATIONS T = Top; M = Middle; B = Bottom; R = Right; L = Left.

BAL= Bridgeman Art Library
RMN= Agence Photographique de la Réunion des Musées Nationaux
TBA = Toucan Books Archive

1 *Young Men Playing Ball*, Musée des Thermes, Rome/Dagli Orti. 2-3 *Procession of the Imperial Court*, Ara Pacis Augustus, Rome/Dagli Orti. 4 *Portrait of Diocletian*, Spink & Son Ltd, London/BAL, TL; *A Baker Serves Bread to Customers*, Museo Nazionale Archeologico, Naples/Scala, TR. 5 *Lady with her Servant*, J. Paul Getty Museum, Malibu/Werner Forman Archive, TL; *Shepherd*, Capitoline Museums, Rome/A. Idini, TR; *Remains of a Meal*, Museo Gregoriano Profano, Vatican, Rome, BL; *Bust of Julius Caesar*, Museo e Gallerie Nazionali di Capodimonte, Naples/Giraudon/BAL, BR. 6 *Romulus and Remus*, Capitoline Museums, Rome/A. Idini. 7 *Eruption of Vesuvius, 1872/* Hulton-Deutsch, TR; *Death of a Young Man*, plaster cast from Pompeii/Erma di Bretschneider, BL; *Front Cover from François Mazor's book on Pompeii/* Toucan Books Archive, BR. 8 *Statue Honouring Celsus' Virtue*, Ephesus/Susan Walker. 9 *Base of Trajan's Column, Rome*, from copy in Victoria & Albert Museum, London. 10-11 Map by Nick Skelton. 12 *Maison Carrée, Nimes, France/*Arcaid/John Edward Linden. 14 *Virgil/*C. M. Dixon. 15 *Portrait of a Couple*, Pompeii, Museo Nazionale Archeologico, Naples/AKG/Eric Lessing. 16 *Statue of a Young Woman*, Musée du Louvre, Paris/Artephot/Takase. 17 *Portrait of Sappho*, Museo Nazionale Archeologico, Naples/Alinari/Giraudon. 18 *Messalina*, Musée du Louvre, Paris/AKG/Eric Lessing, TL; *Finger Ring*, British Museum, London, BR. 19 Illustration by Sarah Kensington. 20 *Seated Couple/*TBA. 21 *Women Selling Poultry*, Museo Torlonia, Rome/Mansell Collection/Alinari, T; *Cameo Portrait of Claudius and Agrippina the Younger, left and Germanicus and Agrippina the Elder*, Kunsthistorisches Museum, Vienna/BAL, B. 22 *Lovers*, from Villa Romana del Casala, Piazza Armerina, Sicily/Dagli Orti. 23 *Family of Augustus*, Ara Pacis Augustus, Rome/Alinari/Giraudon, T; *Portrait of Husband and Wife*, Museo Vaticano, Rome/Scala, B. 24 *Life of a Dead Child*, Giraudon, TL; *Sarcophagus*, Museo Chiaramonti Vaticano, Rome/Scala, BL; *Young Girl and her Cat*, Aquitaine Museum, Bordeaux/Dagli Orti, BR. 25 *Tombs Outside the Walls of Pompeii/*Werner Forman Archive, T; *Relief from Tomb of the Haterii*, Museo Gregoriano Profano, Vaticano, Rome, BR. 26 *Gold Bulla from Pompeii*, Museo e Gallerie Nazionali di Capodimonte, Naples/BAL, T; *Swaddled Baby*, Musée des Antiquités, St. Germain-en-Laye/AKG/Eric Lessing, BR. 27 *Childbirth*, Scavi di Ostia/Werner Forman Archive, TR; *Members of the Imperial Family*, Ara Pacis Augustus, Rome/BPK. 28 *Sundial*, Bulla Regia, Tunisia/Werner Forman Archive, T; *Sundial on a Pillar, Pompeii/* Robert Harding Picture Library/Robert Francis, B. 29 *Children Playing Games*, Museo Lateranense, Rome/Alinari/Giraudon. 31 *Lady at Home with her Servants*, Rheinisches Landesmuseum, Trier. 33 *Via Biberatica*, Forum, Rome/Scala. 34 *Poultry-seller's Shop*, Museo Ostiense Ostia Antica/Scala, T; *Carpenter*, House of the Vettii, Pompeii/Scala, BL. 35 *Horse-drawn Carriage*, Museo della Civilta Romana, Rome/Scala. 36 *Herb-seller's Shop*, Museo Ostiense Ostia Antica/Scala, TR; 36-37 *Patterned Mosaic Floor*, House with Mosaic Hall, Herculaneum/Scala. 38 Illustration by Sarah Kensington, BL; *Portrait of Nero*, Museo di Capitole, Rome/Dagli Orti, T. 39 *Street Scene*, Statens Konstmuseer, Stockholm. 40 *Domestic Scene*, inside Sarcophagus/Rijksmuseum van Ondheden, Leiden. 41 *Grand Hall*, House of the Vettii, Pompeii/Scala. 42 *Three-legged Table*, Home of the Paquio Proculo. 43 *Seaside Villa*, Villa S. Marco/Dagli Orti. 44 *Street in Pompeii/*Lesley and Roy Adkins Picture Library, BL; *Election Candidate Notice/*L'Erma di Bretschneider, TR; *Mosaic of a Dog*, Pompeii/Scala, BR. 45 *Fragment of Wall Graffiti, Sign Outside a Bar*, L'Erma di Bretschneider, T, BR. 46-47 Illustration by Sarah Kensington. 48 Illustration by Sarah Kensington. 49 *Procession of Priests and Senators*, Ara Pacis Augustus, Alinari/Giraudon, T; *Woman Wearing Street-dress*, Museo Chiaramonti Vaticano, Rome/Scala, B. 50 *Woman Pouring Perfume into Flask*, Museo di Therme/Dagli Orti, TL; *Wood and Ivory Toiletry Set*, Museo Nazionale Archeologico, Naples/Dagli Orti, TR; *Gold, Mother-of-pearl Necklace*, Pompeii, Museo Nazionale Archeologico, Naples/E.T. Archive, BL. 51 *Portrait of a Lady*, C.M. Dixon. 52 Museo Capitolini, Rome/Scala, TL, TR; Museo Capitolini, Rome/Dagli Orti, TM; Lauros/Giraudon, TM. 53 *Pulic latrines, Ostia/*C.M. Dixon 54-55 Illustration by Peter Morter. 56 Illustration by Sarah Kensington. 57 *Glassware*, Museo Archeologico, Naples/Dagli Orti, T; *Fruit-gathering*, Musée Antiquités Nationales, St. Germain/Lauros/Giraudon, B. 58-59 *Shop with Food Counter*, Pompeii/Robert Harding Picture Library. 60 *Thrushes/* Lauros/Giraudon. 61 Illustration by Sarah Kensington, BL; *Banquet*, Musée du Louvre, Paris/BAL, TR. 63 *Still Life*, Museo Capodimonte, Naples/Alinari; *Servant carrying Roast Pig/*C.M. Dixon, BL. 64 *Drawing Wine from a Barrel*, Archaeological Museum of Mérida/E.T. Archive. 65 *Shop Selling Cushions/* Alinari/Giraudon. 67 *Interior of the Curia/*C. M. Dixon; *Marcus Aurelius Distributes Family Allowances*, Arch of Constantine, Rome/Alinari, MR. 68 Illustration by Sarah Kensington, BL; *Elector Using Ballot Box*, British Museum, London, TR. 69 Consul of the Republic/Michael Holford. 70 *Butcher's Shop/*Dagli Orti. 71 *Gathering Fruit*, Bardo, Tunisia/C. M. Dixon, TR; *Man with Turkeys*, Imperial Palace, Istanbul/Scala. 72 *Steering and Pulling a Boat*, Musée Lapidaire, Avignon/Dagli Orti. 73 *Knife Seller*, Vatican Museums, Rome, T; *Slave Tag*, British Museum, London, BR. 74 *Trajan's Column/*Robert Harding Picture Library/Adam Woolfitt, BL; *Dacian Wars*, Trajan's Column/Robert Harding Picture Library/Mike Newton, TR. 75 *Merchant Ship*, C. M. Dixon. 76 *Slaves Serving at a Banquet*, Museo Archeologico Nazionale, Naples/Scala. 77 *Tavern Scene*, Diozesanmuseum, Trier/E.T. Archive, T; *Roman Road, Blackstone Edge*, Mick Sharp, BL. 78 *Harbour of Ostia*, Isola Sacra Cemetery, Ostia/Werner Forman Archive. 80-81 Illustration by Sarah Kensington. 82 *Marble Statue of Augustus*, Vatican Museums, Rome/Robert Harding Picture Library, BL. 83 *The Praetorian Guard*, Vatican Museums/Robert Harding Picture Library/John G. Ross. 84 *Battle Scene*, Ludovisi Sarcophagus/Museo Nazionale Romano, Rome/Werner Forman Archive. 85 *A Testudo Formation*, Trajan's Column/C. M. Dixon, T; Illustration by Sarah Kensington, BL; *Sword and its Sheath*, British Museum, London, BR. 86 *Constantine Addresses his Troops/*C. M. Dixon. 87 *Cavalry Officer/*C. M. Dixon. 88 *Bronze Diploma*, British Museum, London, T. 88-89 *Housesteads Fort, Hadrian's Wall/*English Heritage. *90 Fragment of a Letter on Wooden Writing Tablets/*Vindolanda Trust, T; *Roman with Barbarian Prisoner*, C. M. Dixon, B. 91 *Circus Massimo*, Museo Archeologico, Feligno/Scala. 92 *Dice Made of Bone*, E.T. Archive, BL; *Dice Players/*C. M. Dixon, BR. 93 *Children Playing/*Dagli Orti, TL; *Counter and Dice*, Musée Alesia, Alise-Sainte-Reine/Giraudon/BAL, TR. 94 *Cockfight*, Museo Nazionale, Naples/Scala, TL; *Games Judge*, Museo Gregoriano Profano, Vatican, Rome/Scala, BL. 95 *Baths of Neptune*, Ostia/Scala. 96 *Tepidarium*, Pompeii/AKG/Eric Lessing; *Sandales*, Musée Archéologique, Algeria/Dagli Orti, BR. 97 *Silver Vessel*, Museo Nazionale Archeologico, Naples/Dagli Orti, BR; *Bust of Seneca/*C. M. Dixon, TR. 98-99 Illustration by Sarah Kensington. 100 *Actors with their Masks/*C. M. Dixon, BL; *Musicians*, Villa in Nennig, Saarland/AKG/Eric Lessing, TR. 101 *Amphitheatre at Puzzuoli/*Werner Forman Archive. 102 Illustration by Sarah Kensington, BL. 102-103 *Chariot Race*, Musée de la Civilisation Gallo-Romaine, Lyon/AKG/Eric Lessing. 103 *Charioteer/*C. M. Dixon, BR. 104-105 *Rituals*, Musée du Louvre, Paris/Lauros/Giraudon. 104 *Sacrifice Scene*, House of the Vettii, Pompeii/Bulloz, T. 105 *Bacchanalian Revel*, Villa Pamphili, Rome/Michael Holford. 106 *Women Gymnasts*, Villa Romana del Casale Piazza Armerina/Scala, BL; *Chariot Race*, Museo Gregoriano Profano, Vatican, Rome/Scala, T. 107 *Gladiator Fighting a Lion*, Galleria Borghese, Rome/Scala, TR; *Interior of Colosseum, Rome/*Scala, B. 108 Illustration by Sarah Kensington. 109 *Gladiators Killing a Leopard/*C. M. Dixon. 110 *Gladiators*, Museo Nazionale Romano delle Terme, Rome/AKG/Eric Lessing, T; *Bronze Helmet of Thracian Gladiator*, Musée du Louvre, Paris/BAL, B. 111 *Laying Out of the Body*, Museo Gregoriano Profano, Vatican/Werner Forman Archive. 112 *Aesculapius and Hygieia*, National Museums and Galleries on Merseyside (Liverpool Museum). 113 *Roman Baths*, Bath/Arcaid/John E. Linden. 114 *Votive Objects*, British Museum, London/Michael Holford. 115 *Castor-oil Plant*, Österreichische Nationalbibliothek, TL; *Pharmacy Shop/*C. M. Dixon, BR. 116 *Surgeon/*C. M. Dixon. 117 *Medical Instruments*, British Museum, London/Michael Holford, TL; *Aeneas has Arrowhead Removed from his Thigh*, Museo Nazionale Archeologico, Naples/Dagli Orti, MR. 118-119 Illustration by Kevin Goold. 120 *Lar, Household God/* L'Erma di Bretschneider. 121 *Interior of Pantheon, Rome/*Arcaid/John Stuart Miller. 122 Illustration by Sarah Kensington, BL; *Youth Makes an Offering*, Isola Sacra Cemetery/Werner Forman Archive, TR. 123 *Bronze Coin of Janus*, British Museum, London, TR; *Statues of the Vestal Virgins*, Roman Forum/Scala, BM. 124 *Funeral Procession*, Museo Aquilano/Mansell Collection/Alinari. 125 *Making Sacrifice to the Goddess Diana*, Sicily/TBA, T; *Sacrifice of a Bull, a Ram and a Boar/* RMN, B. 126-127 *The Hall of Mysteries*, Pompeii, Museo e Gallerie Nazionale di Capodimonte, Naples/BAL. 128 *Seneca/* TBA, T; *Sacrificial Boy Attendants*, Museo Nazionale Archeologico, Rome/TBA, B. 129 Illustration by Sarah Kensington. 130 *Mithras Slaying the Bull*, Museo Pio-Clemintino, Vatican/Scala. 131 *Priests of Isis*, Herculaneum/C. M. Dixon. 132 *Constantine I/*AKG/Eric Lessing. 133 *View of the Nile*, Museo Archeologico, Palestina/Scala. 134 *Silver Shekel with Head of Hannibal and Elephant*, British Museum, London. 135 *Roman Town of Thogga, Tunisia/*C. M. Dixon. 136 *Triumphant Return of Roman Army from Jerusalem/*Scala, T; *Gaul Enrolled in Roman Army*, Vachères, France/TBA, BR. 137 *Bust of Pompey*, NY Carlsberg Glyptotek, Copenhagen, TL; *Prisoners from Dacia*, British Museum, London, BR. 138-139 Illustration by Kevin Goold. 140 *Walltown Crags, Hadrian's Wall, Northumberland/*Jean Williamson/Mick Sharp, B; *Coin Portraitof Hadrian*, Museum of Antiquities, Newcastle-upon-Tyne/BAL, TL; 141 *Legionary Soldiers*, National Museum of Antiquities of Scotland, ML; *Legionnaire's Bronze Helmet and Shield*, British Museum, London, BR. 142 Illustration by Sarah Kensington. 143 *Two Litigants Argue Before a Judge*, Museo Ostiense, Ostia/Scala. 144 *Ploughing*, Saint-Romain en Gal/RMN, BR. 145 *Village Scene/*L M Trier Th. Zühmer, TL; *Statue of Peasant*, St. Germain-en-Laye, Musée des Antiquités Nationales, MAN 68611/RMN, TR. 146 *Silver Platter*, Mildenhall Treasure, British Museum, London, T; Illustration by Sarah Kensington, BL. 147 *The Pont du Gard*, Nimes, France/Robert Harding Picture Library/Nigel Blythe, T; *Building a Town*, Trajan's Column/Roger-Viollet, B. 148 *Payment of Taxes*, L M Trier Th. Zühmer. 149 *Olive Pressing*, Saint-Romain en Gal/RMN. 150 *View of Rome's Early Buildings*, Museo Gregoriano Profano, Vatican, Rome/Scala, TR; *Manhole Cover*, S. Maria in Cosmediu, Rome/Scala, ML; *Parthenon on Acropolis, Athens/*Dagli Orti, MM; *Temple of Castor and Pollux*, Forum, Rome/Scala, MR; *Assyrian Soldiers at the Time of Ashurbanipal/*TBA, BL. 151 *Serrian Wall, Rome/*Scala, TL; *Scene from a Comedy by Plantus*, Staatliche Museen Preussischer Kulturbesitz, Berlin/BPK, MR; *Quin Shi Huangdi*, Oriental & India Office Collection, British Library, London/Reader's Digest, ML; *Philip II*, British Museum, London, BL. 152 *Bust of Marius and Bust of Sulla/*TBA, TL, TR; *Bust of Ovid/*Alinari, M; *Jerusalem*, Madaba, Jordan/Zev Rodovan, B. 153 *Augustus abd Tiberius*, British Museum, London, T; *Bust of Octavian/*TBA, MR; *Head of Christ*, Catacombe di S. Ermete, Rome/Scala, BL; *Crucifixion of Christ*, British Museum, London, BR. 154 *Claudius*, Kunsthistorisches Museum, Vienna/BAL, TL; *Portraits of Nero and Titus*, Private Collection/BAL, TM, TR; *Temple of Apollo, Pompeii/*Scala, MM; *Fall of Jerusalem*, British Museum, London, BL; *Trajan Talks to Defeated Dacians*, Trajan's Column, Rome/Scala, BR. 155 *Marcus Aurelius/*C. M. Dixon, TL; *Bust of Caracalla*, Musée du Louvre, Paris/BAL, TR; *Gladiator*, British Museum, London, ML; *Arch of Constantine*, Forum, Rome/Hansmann, MR; *Ravenna*, S. Apollinare Nuovo, Ravenna/Scala, BR.

Front cover: Illustration by Sarah Kensington, TL; NY Carlsberg Glyptotek, Copenhagen, ML; Rheinisches Landesmuseum, Trier, MM; Museo Nazionale Archeologico, Naples/Dagli Orti, BL; C.M. Dixon, BM; Musée des Antiquités Nationale, St. Germain/Lauros/Giraudon, BR.

Back cover: BAL, T; Werner Forman Archive, M; Illustration by Sarah Kensington, BL; Dagli Orti, BM; Villa Romana del Casale Piazza Armerina/Scala, BR.

The editors are grateful to the following publishers for their kind permission to quote passages from the books below: English Heritage, *Food and Cooking in Roman Britain*, Jane Renfrew, 1985; Harvard University Press, *Epigrams* by Martial, translated by D. R. Shakleton Bailey, 1993; Hogarth Press, *The Romans and their Gods*, R. M. Ogilvie, 1986; Oxford University Press, *As the Romans Did*, Jo-Ann Shelton, 1988; Penguin, *Epigrams* by Martial, translated by James Michie, 1973; Penguin, *Letters from a Stoic* by Seneca, translated by Robin Campbell, 1969; Penguin, *The Annals of Imperial Rome* by Tacitus, translated by Michael Grant, 1989; Penguin, *The Letters of the Younger Pliny*, translated by Betty Radice, 1963; Penguin, *The Satyricon* by Petronius, translated by J. P. Sullivan, 1986; Penguin, *The Twelve Caesars* by Suetronius, translated by Robert Graves, 1979; Rider Books, *The Roman Cookery of Apicius*, translated by John Edwards.